I0489886

Zoho User Manual for Businesses

By

Jaiden Dev

TABLE OF CONTENTS

D. Zoho Desk

1. Features

2. Setup and Configuration

3. Managing Support Tickets

4. Knowledge Base

5. Reports and Analytics

E. Zoho Projects

1. Features

2. Setup and Configuration

3. Managing Tasks and Milestones

4. Time Tracking

5. Reports and Analytics

IV. ADVANCED FEATURES AND CUSTOMIZATIONS

A. Zoho Creator

B. Zoho Flow

D. Training and Certification

VIII. CONCLUSION

I. INTRODUCTION

A. About Zoho

Zoho Corporation is an Indian multinational technology company that offers a suite of software applications to help businesses manage their operations. The company was founded in 1996 by Sridhar Vembu and Tony Thomas in Chennai, India, and has since grown to become one of the largest software companies in India. Zoho's products are used by millions of users across the globe and range from customer relationship management (CRM) software to email marketing tools and project management software.

Zoho's product suite includes over 45 web applications that help businesses manage their operations. These applications are designed to help businesses automate their processes, increase productivity, and improve their customer engagement. Some of the most popular Zoho products include:

- Zoho CRM: Zoho's customer relationship management software helps businesses manage their customer interactions and sales pipelines. The software allows businesses to track leads, monitor sales activities, and automate sales processes.

- Zoho Books: Zoho Books is an accounting software that helps businesses manage their finances. The software includes features such as invoicing, expense tracking, and inventory management.

- Zoho Projects: Zoho Projects is a project management software that helps businesses manage their projects from start to finish. The software includes features such as task management, Gantt charts, and team collaboration tools.

- Zoho Creator: Zoho Creator is a low-code platform that allows businesses to build custom applications without any coding knowledge. The platform includes drag-and-drop tools and pre-built templates to make app development faster and easier.

- Zoho Campaigns: Zoho Campaigns is an email marketing software that helps businesses create and send email campaigns. The software includes features such as email templates, A/B testing, and analytics to help businesses improve their email marketing strategies.

Zoho's products are known for their affordability and ease of use. The company offers a range of pricing options, including a free plan for many of its products, which makes it accessible to businesses of all sizes. Zoho also offers a suite of mobile apps, which allows users to access their Zoho applications from anywhere, at any time.

Zoho has received numerous awards for its products and services, including the PCMag Editor's Choice award for Best CRM in 2021 and the Gartner Peer Insights Customers' Choice award for CRM Lead Management in 2021. The company has also been recognized for its corporate social responsibility initiatives, including its efforts to reduce its carbon footprint and its support of education initiatives in rural India.

B. Benefits of using Zoho for Businesses

Zoho is a cloud-based software suite that offers a wide range of applications designed to help businesses manage their operations more efficiently. From customer relationship management to accounting, marketing automation, project management, and more, Zoho provides a comprehensive suite of tools to help businesses streamline their processes and boost productivity. In this section, we will explore the benefits of using Zoho for businesses.

1. All-in-One Platform

One of the primary benefits of using Zoho is that it is an all-in-one platform that provides a range of business applications. Instead of having to use different software for different tasks, businesses can use Zoho for a wide range of functions such as accounting, project management, customer relationship management, email marketing, and more. This helps to streamline operations and eliminates the need for multiple software subscriptions.

2. Cost-Effective

Zoho is a cost-effective solution for businesses of all sizes. Unlike other software suites that require significant upfront costs, Zoho offers a variety of pricing plans, including a free plan with limited features, making it an accessible solution for businesses on a budget. Even its paid plans are affordable and offer significant value for the price.

4. Easy to Use

Zoho is designed to be user-friendly, making it easy for businesses to adopt and integrate into their operations. With intuitive interfaces and easy-to-navigate menus, businesses can quickly learn how to use the various applications and start using them right away. Additionally, Zoho offers comprehensive documentation and tutorials to help users learn and troubleshoot any issues they may encounter.

4. Customizable

Zoho is highly customizable, which allows businesses to tailor the software to their specific needs. Users can easily create custom workflows, fields, and reports to suit their unique business processes. Additionally, Zoho integrates with a wide range of third-party applications, allowing businesses to customize their suite even further.

5. Mobile-Friendly

Zoho is designed to be mobile-friendly, which means that businesses can access and use the software from their mobile devices. This is particularly beneficial for businesses with remote or field-based employees who need to access data and information while on the go. The mobile app offers all the same features as the desktop version, making it a convenient solution for businesses that need to stay connected while on the move.

6. Security

Zoho takes security seriously, and the software suite includes a range of security features to protect sensitive business data. This includes SSL encryption, two-factor authentication, and regular backups of all data. Additionally, Zoho complies with various data protection regulations, including GDPR, HIPAA, and SOC 2.

7. Integration

Zoho integrates seamlessly with other applications and platforms, including Google Workspace, Microsoft 365, and Zapier. This allows businesses to connect their various tools and streamline their operations even further. Additionally, Zoho offers an API that allows developers to build custom integrations, making it a versatile solution for businesses with unique needs.

Overall, Zoho is a powerful and comprehensive software suite that offers a wide range of benefits for businesses. From its cost-effective pricing plans to its user-friendly interface, customizable workflows, mobile-friendly design, and robust security features, Zoho provides businesses with everything they need to streamline their operations and boost productivity. If you're looking for a versatile, all-in-one solution for your business, Zoho is definitely worth considering.

C. Getting Started

Zoho is a suite of web-based software applications designed to help businesses manage their operations more efficiently. It offers a wide range of applications, including CRM, project management, invoicing, email marketing, and more.

If you are new to Zoho, getting started may seem daunting at first. However, the following steps will guide you on how to get started with Zoho.

Step 1: Sign up for a Zoho account

The first step to getting started with Zoho is to sign up for a Zoho account. To do this, go to the Zoho website and click on the "Sign Up" button. You will be prompted to enter your email address and create a password. Once you have done this, click on the "Sign Up" button again to complete the registration process.

Step 2: Choose the Zoho application(s) you want to use

After you have signed up for a Zoho account, the next step is to choose the Zoho application(s) you want to use. Zoho offers a wide range of applications, so take some time to explore the various options available and decide which ones are most suitable for your business.

Step 3: Customize your Zoho account

Once you have chosen the Zoho application(s) you want to use, the next step is to customize your Zoho account. This involves adding your company information, configuring your settings, and setting up your preferences.

Step 4: Import your data

If you are migrating from another software application or system, the next step is to import your data into Zoho. Zoho offers data migration tools for most of its applications, so be sure to take advantage of these tools to make the migration process as smooth as possible.

Step 5: Train your team

After you have set up your Zoho account and imported your data, the next step is to train your team on how to use Zoho. This involves showing them how to navigate the system, how to perform various tasks, and how to access support if they need it.

Step 6: Integrate Zoho with other applications

Zoho offers integrations with a wide range of other software applications, including Google Apps, Microsoft Office, and many others. By integrating Zoho with other applications, you can streamline your workflows and make your business more efficient.

Overall, getting started with Zoho involves signing up for a Zoho account, choosing the Zoho application(s) you want to use, customizing your Zoho account, importing your data, training your team, and integrating Zoho with other applications. By following these steps, you can make the most of Zoho and enjoy its many benefits for your business.

II. SETTING UP YOUR ZOHO ACCOUNT

A. Creating an Account

Zoho is a cloud-based software company that provides a suite of online applications, including email, project management, CRM, and accounting. Creating an account on Zoho is easy and straightforward. In this guide, we will take you through the steps involved in creating a new account on Zoho.

Step 1: Go to the Zoho Website

The first step is to navigate to the Zoho website. You can do this by typing "www.zoho.com" into your web browser or by clicking on the link provided in your search engine results.

Step 2: Click on the "Sign Up" Button

Once you are on the Zoho website, locate the "Sign Up" button, which is usually located at the top of the page. Click on the button to proceed to the next step.

Step 3: Choose the Zoho Application

After clicking on the "Sign Up" button, you will be redirected to a page where you can choose the Zoho application you want to sign up for. Zoho offers a wide range of applications, including Zoho Mail, Zoho CRM, Zoho Projects, Zoho Books, and many more. Select the application you want to sign up for by clicking on its icon.

Step 4: Enter Your Details

Once you have selected the Zoho application you want to sign up for, you will be taken to a registration page. Here, you will be required to provide some basic information to create your account. The information you will be asked to provide includes your name, email address, and a password.

Step 5: Verify Your Email Address

After entering your details, Zoho will send you an email to verify your email address. Check your email inbox and click on the verification link to complete the registration process.

Step 6: Complete Your Profile

Once you have verified your email address, you will be taken to your Zoho profile page. Here, you can complete your profile by adding additional information such as your business name, website URL, and contact details.

Step 7: Explore Zoho

Now that you have successfully created your account, you can start exploring the features and functionalities of your Zoho application. You can start using your Zoho app to manage your emails, CRM, projects, and more.

By following the steps outlined above, you can create a new account and start using Zoho to manage your business operations.

B. Adding Users

Zoho is a cloud-based software suite that offers a range of business applications. Zoho offers a user management system that allows administrators to create, manage and control user access to the various applications offered by Zoho.

Adding users on Zoho is a simple process that can be completed in a few steps. The process involves creating a user account, assigning user roles, and granting access to the desired applications.

To add a user to Zoho, follow the steps below:

Step 1: Log in to your Zoho account

To add a user, you need to log in to your Zoho account. Once you are logged in, navigate to the user management section of your Zoho dashboard.

Step 2: Create a user account

To create a user account, click on the "Add User" button. This will bring up a form where you can enter the user's details, such as name, email address, and password.

Step 3: Assign user roles

Zoho offers various user roles that can be assigned to users depending on their level of access to your Zoho applications. The available user roles include administrator, manager, user, and guest.

Administrators have full access to all the features and settings in your Zoho account. Managers have access to specific applications and can manage users and settings for those applications. Users have access to specific applications, and guests have limited access to view data in specific applications.

Select the appropriate user role for the user you are adding.

Step 4: Grant access to applications

After assigning a user role, you need to grant access to the applications the user needs to use. To do this, navigate to the application settings section of your Zoho dashboard.

Select the application you want to grant access to and add the user to the list of authorized users for that application. You can grant access to multiple applications for a user by repeating this step for each application.

Step 5: Save changes

Once you have added the user, assigned a user role, and granted access to the desired applications, click on the "Save" button to save your changes.

That's it! You have successfully added a user to your Zoho account.

Overall, adding users on Zoho is a simple process that involves creating a user account, assigning user roles, and granting access to the desired applications. By following the above steps, you can easily add users and manage their access to your Zoho applications.

C. Managing Roles and Permissions

Zoho is a popular cloud-based suite of productivity and business applications used by organizations of all sizes. One of the key features of Zoho is the ability to manage roles and permissions, which allows you to control who has access to specific features and data within the platform. In this section, we'll take a closer look at how to manage roles and permissions in Zoho.

Understanding Roles in Zoho

Before we dive into managing roles and permissions in Zoho, it's important to understand what roles are and how they work within the platform. In Zoho, a role is a predefined set of permissions that determines what a user can and cannot do within the system.

For example, Zoho has several built-in roles such as Administrator, Marketing Manager, Sales Manager, and Support Agent. Each of these roles has its own set of permissions that determine what the user can access and do within the platform.

You can also create custom roles in Zoho to further refine the permissions for specific users or groups of users. Custom roles can be created by combining the permissions of existing roles or by creating a new set of permissions from scratch.

1. Managing Roles in Zoho

To manage roles in Zoho, you'll need to have Administrator or Super Administrator permissions. Here's how to get started:

1. Log in to your Zoho account and go to the "Settings" menu.
2. Click on "Security" and then "Roles" to access the role management screen.
3. From here, you can view the list of existing roles in your organization and their associated permissions.
4. To create a new role, click on the "New Role" button and give the role a name and description.
5. Next, select the permissions that you want to assign to the role by clicking on the checkboxes next to each permission.
6. Once you've selected the permissions, click on the "Save" button to create the new role.

7. You can also edit existing roles in Zoho by clicking on the role name and then selecting the permissions that you want to add or remove. When you're done, click on the "Save" button to update the role.

Assigning Roles to Users

Once you've created and configured your roles in Zoho, you'll need to assign them to specific users or groups of users. Here's how to do it:

1. Go to the "Users" tab in the "Security" menu.
2. Select the user that you want to assign a role to.
3. Click on the "Roles" tab and then click on the "Add Role" button.
4. Select the role that you want to assign to the user and click on the "Save" button.
5. You can also assign roles to multiple users at once by selecting them from the list and then clicking on the "Add Role" button. This is useful if you want to assign the same role to a group of users.

2. Managing Permissions in Zoho

In addition to managing roles, you can also manage permissions directly in Zoho. Permissions allow you to control access to specific features and data within the platform.

To manage permissions in Zoho, follow these steps:

1. Go to the "Settings" menu and click on "Security."
2. Click on "Permissions" to access the permission management screen.
3. From here, you can view the list of existing permissions in your organization and their associated roles.
4. To create a new permission, click on the "New Permission" button and give the permission a name and description.
5. Next, select the roles that you want to assign the permission to by clicking on the checkboxes next to each role.
6. Once you've selected the roles, click on the "Save" button to create the new permission.
7. You can also edit existing permissions in Zoho by clicking on the permission name and then selecting the roles that you want to add or

remove. When you're done, click on the "Save" button to update the permission.

Best Practices for Managing Roles and Permissions in Zoho

Here are some best practices to keep in mind when managing roles and permissions in Zoho:

- Start with a clear understanding of what data and features each user or group of users needs access to. This will help you create roles and permissions that are tailored to their needs.
- Regularly review and update your roles and permissions to ensure that they are still appropriate for each user or group of users. This will help you maintain security and avoid granting unnecessary access.
- Limit the number of users with Administrator or Super Administrator permissions to reduce the risk of unauthorized changes to your Zoho account.
- Be careful when granting permissions to custom roles, as these can override the

permissions of built-in roles and lead to unintended consequences.

- Use Zoho's audit trail feature to monitor changes made to roles and permissions in your account.

By following these best practices, you can help ensure that your Zoho account remains secure and that users only have access to the data and features they need to do their jobs.

Overall, managing roles and permissions in Zoho is an important aspect of ensuring the security and effectiveness of your organization's use of the platform. By understanding the different types of roles and permissions in Zoho, and following best practices for managing them, you can help ensure that your users have the right access to the right features and data, while minimizing the risk of unauthorized access or unintended consequences.

D. Customizing Your Dashboard

Zoho is a powerful and versatile cloud-based business software suite that offers a wide range of applications to help businesses of all sizes manage their operations effectively. One of the standout features of Zoho is its dashboard customization options. With Zoho, users can customize their dashboard to suit their specific needs and preferences, making it easier to stay on top of important business data and metrics.

In this section, we will take a closer look at how to customize your dashboard on Zoho.

1. Choose your Dashboard Layout:

The first step in customizing your dashboard is to choose the layout that best suits your needs. Zoho offers several different dashboard layouts to choose from, each with its own unique set of features and benefits. To select a dashboard layout, simply click on the "Customize" button located at the top right corner of your screen, then select "Dashboard Layout." From there, you can choose the layout that works best for you.

2. Add Widgets:

Once you have selected your dashboard layout, you can start adding widgets to your dashboard. Widgets are small, customizable modules that display specific types of data and metrics. To add a widget, simply click on the "Add Widget" button located at the top right corner of your screen, then select the widget you want to add.

There are many different types of widgets to choose from in Zoho, including:

- Analytics widgets that display key performance indicators (KPIs) and other important business metrics
- Calendar widgets that display upcoming events and deadlines
- Chat widgets that allow you to communicate with team members and clients
- Sales widgets that track your sales pipeline and provide insights into your sales performance

- Social media widgets that display your social media activity and engagement metrics
- Support widgets that track your customer support tickets and response times

3. Customize Your Widgets:

Once you have added a widget to your dashboard, you can customize it to display the data and metrics that are most important to you. To customize a widget, simply click on the "Settings" button located at the top right corner of the widget. From there, you can select the data source, set up filters, and choose the display options for the widget.

4. Organize Your Widgets:

As you add more widgets to your dashboard, it's important to organize them in a way that makes sense for your business. Zoho makes it easy to rearrange your widgets by simply clicking and dragging them to the desired location on your dashboard.

5. Save Your Dashboard:

Once you have customized your dashboard to your liking, it's important to save your changes. To save your dashboard, simply click on the "Save" button located at the top right corner of your screen. You can also choose to share your dashboard with other team members or set it as your default dashboard.

Overall, customizing your dashboard on Zoho is a great way to stay on top of important business data and metrics. By choosing the right dashboard layout, adding relevant widgets, customizing your widgets, organizing your dashboard, and saving your changes, you can create a personalized dashboard that helps you make informed business decisions and stay ahead of the competition.

E. Integrating with Other Applications

Zoho is a suite of cloud-based business applications that allows businesses to manage their operations online. With over 50+ applications in its suite, Zoho provides businesses with a wide range of tools for managing their operations. One of the key features of Zoho is its ability to integrate with other applications.

Integrating with other applications on Zoho allows businesses to streamline their operations and automate their workflows. In this section, we will discuss how to integrate with other applications on Zoho, the benefits of integration, and some examples of popular integrations.

How to Integrate with Other Applications on Zoho

i. Integrating with other applications on Zoho is a straightforward process that involves the following steps:

ii.   Choose the application you want to integrate with: Zoho offers a wide range of applications that can be integrated with other applications. Choose the application you want to integrate with based on your business needs.

iii.   Enable the integration: Once you have chosen the application you want to integrate with, you will need to enable the integration. This involves providing the necessary credentials and permissions to allow Zoho to access the other application.

iv.   Configure the integration: After enabling the integration, you will need to configure it. This involves setting up the integration to work the way you want it to.

v.   Test the integration: Once you have configured the integration, you will need to test it to ensure it is working correctly. This involves running some test transactions to ensure the data is being transferred correctly between the two applications.

vi. Monitor the integration: After the integration is up and running, you will need to monitor it to ensure it continues to work correctly. This involves checking for errors and resolving any issues that arise.

Benefits of Integrating with Other Applications on Zoho

Integrating with other applications on Zoho offers several benefits to businesses, including:

i. Streamlining operations: Integrating with other applications allows businesses to streamline their operations by automating their workflows. This can save time and reduce errors.

ii. Increased efficiency: Integrating with other applications can increase efficiency by reducing the need for manual data entry and reducing the risk of errors.

iii. Improved data accuracy: Integrating with other applications can improve data accuracy by reducing the risk of errors caused by manual data entry.

iv. Better data visibility: Integrating with other applications can provide better data visibility by consolidating data from multiple sources into a single location.

v. Improved customer experience: Integrating with other applications can improve the customer experience by providing a seamless experience across multiple platforms.

Examples of Popular Integrations on Zoho

i. Zoho CRM and Zoho Campaigns: Integrating Zoho CRM with Zoho Campaigns allows businesses to manage their customer relationships and email marketing campaigns in a single platform.

ii. Zoho Books and PayPal: Integrating Zoho Books with PayPal allows businesses to accept payments online and manage their finances in a single platform.

iii. Zoho Projects and Google Drive: Integrating Zoho Projects with Google Drive allows businesses to collaborate on projects and share documents in a single platform.

iv. Zoho Desk and Salesforce: Integrating Zoho Desk with Salesforce allows businesses to manage customer support tickets and customer relationships in a single platform.

v. Zoho Inventory and Amazon: Integrating Zoho Inventory with Amazon allows businesses to manage their inventory and sales on Amazon in a single platform.

Overall, integrating with other applications on Zoho is a powerful tool for businesses looking to streamline their operations and improve efficiency. By integrating with other applications, businesses can automate their workflows, improve data accuracy, and provide a better customer experience. Zoho offers a wide range of applications that can be integrated with other applications, allowing businesses to choose the integrations that best fit their needs.

III. ZOHO APPS FOR BUSINESSES

A. Zoho CRM

1. Features

Zoho CRM is a customer relationship management software that helps businesses to manage their interactions with customers and leads. It offers a wide range of features to help businesses to manage their sales, marketing, customer support, and other activities. In this section, we will explore the features of Zoho CRM in detail.

1. Contact Management:

Zoho CRM offers a comprehensive contact management system that helps businesses to manage their contacts effectively. The system allows businesses to store customer and lead information in a central location, including contact details, company information, social media profiles, and more. It also provides an easy way to categorize contacts and segment them based on various criteria, including location, industry, company size, and more.

2. Sales Automation:

Zoho CRM offers a range of tools to help businesses automate their sales processes. It includes features like lead scoring, sales forecasting, deal management, and more. The system allows businesses to create custom sales workflows to streamline their sales processes and improve efficiency.

3. Marketing Automation:

Zoho CRM also offers a range of marketing automation tools to help businesses streamline their marketing activities. It includes features like email marketing, social media integration, landing page creation, and more. The system allows businesses to create personalized campaigns to engage with customers and improve conversion rates.

4. Customer Support:

Zoho CRM includes a comprehensive customer support system that helps businesses to manage customer inquiries and support requests. It includes features like ticket management, knowledge base creation, and more. The system allows businesses to provide timely and effective support to their customers, improving customer satisfaction and loyalty.

5. Reporting and Analytics:

Zoho CRM provides a range of reporting and analytics tools that help businesses to track their performance and make data-driven decisions. It includes features like dashboards, custom reports, and more. The system allows businesses to track key metrics like sales revenue, conversion rates, customer satisfaction, and more.

6. Mobile App:

Zoho CRM offers a mobile app that allows businesses to access their CRM data from anywhere, anytime. The app includes features like contact management, deal management, lead management, and more. It also provides real-time alerts and notifications to keep businesses informed about important events and activities.

7. Integrations:

Zoho CRM integrates with a wide range of third-party tools and applications, including email clients, social media platforms, marketing automation tools, and more. The system allows businesses to streamline their workflows and improve efficiency by connecting their CRM with other business tools.

Overall, Zoho CRM offers a comprehensive set of features to help businesses manage their sales, marketing, customer support, and other activities. Its contact management, sales automation, marketing automation, customer support, reporting and analytics, mobile app, and integrations make it a powerful tool for businesses of all sizes.

2. Setup and Configuration

Zoho CRM is a powerful customer relationship management system that helps businesses manage their sales, marketing, and customer service activities. Setting up and configuring Zoho CRM can be a daunting task, but with the right guidance and tools, it can be a smooth and seamless process. In this section, I will guide you through the process of setting up and configuring Zoho CRM.

Step 1: Sign up for Zoho CRM

The first step in setting up Zoho CRM is to sign up for an account. You can do this by visiting the Zoho CRM website and clicking on the "Sign Up Now" button. You will then be prompted to enter your email address and password. Once you have done this, click on the "Sign Up" button to create your account.

Step 2: Customize Your Account

Once you have created your account, you will be prompted to customize your account. This includes selecting your industry, the size of your organization, and your preferred language. You can also choose whether to use Zoho CRM's standard edition or professional edition, depending on your needs.

Step 3: Set Up Your Organization

The next step is to set up your organization within Zoho CRM. This includes entering information such as your company name, address, and phone number. You can also add other details such as your logo, social media profiles, and website address.

Step 4: Import Data

If you have existing customer data, you can import it into Zoho CRM using a variety of methods. You can import data from Excel spreadsheets, CSV files, or even directly from other CRM systems. This will help you to get started with Zoho CRM quickly and easily.

Step 5: Set Up Users

Once you have imported your data, you can set up users within Zoho CRM. This includes adding your sales team, marketing team, and customer service team. You can also assign roles and permissions to each user, depending on their job responsibilities.

Step 6: Customize Your Layout

Zoho CRM allows you to customize the layout of your dashboard to suit your needs. You can add or remove widgets, change the color scheme, and even add your own branding. This will help you to create a personalized workspace that is tailored to your business needs.

Step 7: Set Up Automation Rules

Automation rules can help you to streamline your sales and marketing processes within Zoho CRM. You can create rules that automatically assign leads to sales reps, send follow-up emails, and even trigger alerts when certain conditions are met.

This will help you to save time and increase efficiency within your organization.

Step 8: Set Up Integrations

Zoho CRM integrates with a wide range of third-party apps and services. This includes popular tools such as Mailchimp, Zapier, and QuickBooks. Setting up integrations will help you to streamline your workflows and reduce the need for manual data entry.

Step 9: Customize Your Sales Process

Zoho CRM allows you to customize your sales process to suit your specific needs. You can create custom stages, add fields, and even create custom modules. This will help you to create a sales process that is tailored to your business needs.

Step 10: Train Your Team

Finally, it is important to train your team on how to use Zoho CRM effectively. This includes showing them how to use the various features and tools, as well as providing ongoing support and training. By doing this, you can ensure that your team is fully equipped to use Zoho CRM to its full potential.

In conclusion, setting up and configuring Zoho CRM can be a complex process, but by following these ten steps, you can ensure that the process is as smooth and seamless as possible. By taking the time to customize your account, import your data, set up users, customize your layout, set up automation rules and integrations, customize your sales process, and train your team, you can get the most out of Zoho CRM and improve your business operations.

It is important to note that Zoho CRM is a powerful tool that can help you to streamline your business processes and improve customer relationships. However, it is also important to ensure that your team is fully trained and equipped to use the tool effectively. By providing ongoing support and training, you can help your team to get the most out of Zoho CRM and improve your overall business operations.

In addition to the steps outlined above, Zoho CRM also offers a range of other features and tools that can help you to improve your business processes. These include lead scoring, email tracking, sales forecasting, and more. By taking advantage of these features, you can gain deeper insights into your customers and make more informed business decisions.

Overall, setting up and configuring Zoho CRM is a crucial step in improving your business operations and customer relationships. By following the steps outlined above and taking advantage of the features and tools offered by Zoho CRM, you can streamline your workflows, improve your sales and marketing processes, and ultimately grow your business.

3. Managing Leads and Contacts

Zoho CRM is a powerful Customer Relationship Management (CRM) software that helps businesses to streamline their sales process, automate their marketing campaigns, and manage their customer interactions effectively. One of the core features of Zoho CRM is the ability to manage leads and contacts. In this section, we'll explore how to effectively manage leads and contacts using Zoho CRM.

Understanding Leads and Contacts

Before we dive into how to manage leads and contacts in Zoho CRM, it's essential to understand what leads and contacts are. In Zoho CRM, a lead is a potential customer who has shown interest in your product or service but hasn't yet made a purchase. A contact, on the other hand, is a customer who has already made a purchase or has an existing business relationship with your company.

Managing Leads in Zoho CRM

Managing leads in Zoho CRM involves capturing leads, nurturing them, and converting them into customers. Here are the steps to manage leads effectively using Zoho CRM:

1. Capture Leads

The first step in managing leads is to capture them. Zoho CRM provides various ways to capture leads, including:

Web-to-Lead Forms: You can create a custom form using Zoho CRM's drag-and-drop form builder and embed it on your website. When a user fills the form, their details will be captured in Zoho CRM as a lead.

Importing Leads: If you have a list of leads in a CSV or Excel file, you can import them into Zoho CRM in bulk.

Lead Generation: You can also use Zoho CRM's lead generation tools, such as LinkedIn Sales Navigator integration, to find and capture new leads.

2. Qualify Leads

Not all leads are created equal. Some may be more interested in your product than others. Zoho CRM's lead scoring feature can help you prioritize leads based on their level of engagement with your company. You can assign scores to leads based on their website activity, email opens, clicks, and other criteria. This will help you identify the most engaged leads and prioritize them for follow-up.

3. Nurture Leads

Once you've identified your most engaged leads, it's essential to nurture them by providing them with relevant content and engaging with them through email, social media, or phone calls. Zoho CRM's marketing automation tools can help you create targeted email campaigns and track the engagement of your leads.

4. Convert Leads

The ultimate goal of managing leads is to convert them into customers. Zoho CRM's sales automation tools can help you streamline your sales process and convert leads into customers faster. You can create custom sales pipelines, track deal stages, and automate follow-up tasks to ensure that no lead falls through the cracks.

Managing Contacts in Zoho CRM

Managing contacts in Zoho CRM involves organizing your existing customers and maintaining a good relationship with them. Here are the steps to manage contacts effectively using Zoho CRM:

1. Import Contacts

If you have a list of existing customers, you can import them into Zoho CRM as contacts. You can also manually add contacts one by one.

2. Categorize Contacts

Once you've imported your contacts, you can categorize them based on their demographics, industry, or any other criteria that are relevant to your business. This will help you segment your contact list and create targeted marketing campaigns.

3. Maintain Contact Information

It's essential to keep your contact information up to date. Zoho CRM allows you to store all contact information, including emails, phone numbers, addresses, and social media profiles, in one place. You can also set up reminders to follow up with contacts and keep track of their engagement with your company.

4. Engage with Contacts

Maintaining a good relationship with your contacts is crucial for customer retention and repeat business. Zoho CRM's customer engagement tools can help you stay in touch with your contacts and provide them with personalized experiences. You can create targeted email campaigns, send SMS messages, and track their engagement with your company.

5. Track Customer Interactions

Zoho CRM allows you to track all customer interactions, including calls, emails, and social media interactions, in one place. This will help you understand your customers' needs better and provide them with better service.

6. Upsell and Cross-sell

Once you've established a good relationship with your contacts, you can upsell and cross-sell your products or services to them. Zoho CRM's sales automation tools can help you identify opportunities for upselling and cross-selling and automate the process to ensure that your contacts receive the right offer at the right time.

Overall, Effective lead and contact management is essential for the success of any business. Zoho CRM provides powerful tools to help you capture, qualify, nurture, and convert leads into customers, as well as organize and maintain good relationships with your existing customers. By following the steps outlined in this section, you can leverage Zoho CRM's features to streamline your sales process, automate your marketing campaigns, and provide your customers with personalized experiences.

4. Creating Sales Pipeline

Zoho CRM is a powerful Customer Relationship Management tool that can help you manage your sales pipeline. A sales pipeline is a visual representation of the sales process. It is a way of tracking the progress of a sale from start to finish. In this section, we will discuss how to create a sales pipeline with Zoho CRM.

Step 1: Define Your Sales Process

The first step in creating a sales pipeline with Zoho CRM is to define your sales process. This includes identifying the stages of your sales cycle, the tasks that need to be completed at each stage, and the criteria that determine when a lead moves from one stage to the next.

Some common stages in a sales process include:

- Lead generation
- Qualification
- Needs analysis
- Proposal/quote
- Negotiation
- Close

Once you have defined your sales process, you can create custom fields in Zoho CRM to track the progress of your leads through each stage.

Step 2: Set Up Your Sales Pipeline

To create a sales pipeline in Zoho CRM, you need to set up a custom module. A module is a container for storing data related to a specific area of your business. In this case, we will create a custom module for our sales pipeline.

To create a custom module, follow these steps:

- Go to the Zoho CRM homepage and click on the "Settings" icon in the top right corner.

- Click on "Modules" under the "Customization" section.
- Click on the "Create Module" button in the top right corner.
- Enter a name for your module (e.g., "Sales Pipeline") and select the "Leads" module as the parent module.
- Click on the "Save" button.
- Once you have created your custom module, you can add custom fields to track the progress of your leads through each stage of the sales process.

Step 3: Add Custom Fields

Custom fields are a way to store additional information about your leads. In Zoho CRM, you can create custom fields to track the progress of your leads through each stage of the sales process.

To create a custom field, follow these steps:

- Go to the "Settings" page and click on "Fields" under the "Customization" section.

- Click on the "Create Field" button in the top right corner.
- Select the type of field you want to create (e.g., dropdown, checkbox, date, etc.) and enter a name for your field.
- Choose which module you want to add the field to (e.g., "Sales Pipeline") and select the appropriate options for the field.
- Click on the "Save" button.
- Repeat this process for each stage of your sales process.

Step 4: Create Sales Pipeline Views

Once you have added custom fields to your sales pipeline module, you can create views to track your leads through each stage of the sales process.

To create a view, follow these steps:

- Go to the "Sales Pipeline" module and click on the "Views" tab.
- Click on the "Create View" button in the top right corner.

- Enter a name for your view (e.g., "Lead Generation") and select the appropriate options for the view.
- Click on the "Save" button.
- Repeat this process for each stage of your sales process.

Step 5: Add Leads to Your Sales Pipeline

To add a lead to your sales pipeline, follow these steps:

- Go to the "Leads" module and select the lead you want to add to your sales pipeline.
- Click on the "Edit" button.
- Select the appropriate options for each custom field in your sales pipeline module.
- Click on the "Save"

Once you have added a lead to your sales pipeline module, you can view it in the appropriate view. For example, if you have a lead in the "Lead Generation" stage, you can view it in the "Lead Generation" view.

Step 6: Track Your Leads Through Each Stage

As your leads progress through each stage of the sales process, you can update their information in your sales pipeline module. For example, if a lead moves from the "Lead Generation" stage to the "Qualification" stage, you can update their information in the "Qualification" view.

To update a lead's information, follow these steps:

- Go to the "Sales Pipeline" module and select the lead you want to update.
- Click on the "Edit" button.
- Update the appropriate fields with the lead's new information.
- Click on the "Save" button.

Step 7: Monitor Your Sales Pipeline

One of the benefits of using Zoho CRM to create a sales pipeline is the ability to monitor your pipeline in real-time. You can see how many leads are in each stage of the sales process, which leads are stuck in a particular stage, and which leads are likely to close.

To monitor your sales pipeline, follow these steps:

- Go to the "Sales Pipeline" module and select the appropriate view.
- Use the filter and sort options to view the leads in the way you want.
- Use the charts and graphs to analyze your pipeline and identify areas for improvement.

Step 8: Automate Your Sales Pipeline

Zoho CRM also allows you to automate your sales pipeline. You can create workflows that automatically update a lead's information based on certain triggers, such as when a lead is moved to a particular stage.

To create a workflow, follow these steps:

- Go to the "Settings" page and click on "Workflows" under the "Automation" section.
- Click on the "Create Workflow" button in the top right corner.
- Select the module you want to create the workflow for (e.g., "Sales Pipeline") and choose the appropriate trigger.
- Add actions to the workflow, such as updating a field or sending an email.
- Click on the "Save" button.

By automating your sales pipeline, you can save time and ensure that your leads are always up-to-date.

Overall, creating a sales pipeline with Zoho CRM can help you manage your sales process more effectively. By defining your sales process, setting up your sales pipeline, adding custom fields, creating views, adding leads, tracking your leads through each stage, monitoring your sales pipeline, and automating your sales pipeline, you can improve your sales performance and close more deals.

5. Reports and Analytics

Zoho CRM is a powerful customer relationship management (CRM) software that allows businesses to manage their customer data and interactions more efficiently. One of the key features of Zoho CRM is its reporting and analytics capabilities, which provide businesses with insights into their sales performance, customer behavior, and overall business operations.

Reports in Zoho CRM can be customized to meet the specific needs of a business. The software provides a range of pre-built reports that cover common business metrics, such as lead sources, sales by product or service, and deal stages. These reports can be customized by adding or removing columns, changing the sorting order, and filtering data based on specific criteria.

Zoho CRM also provides the ability to create custom reports from scratch, allowing businesses to analyze their data in more depth. Custom reports can be created using a drag-and-drop interface, which makes it easy to add and organize data fields. Reports can be filtered based on a range of criteria, such as date range, owner, stage, and status.

Zoho CRM also provides a range of analytics tools that help businesses gain insights into their data. For example, the software provides a dashboard that displays key performance indicators (KPIs), such as revenue, sales pipeline, and customer engagement. The dashboard can be customized to display the metrics that are most important to a business and can be accessed from anywhere with an internet connection.

In addition to the dashboard, Zoho CRM provides a range of other analytics tools, including:

1. Forecasting: Zoho CRM provides a sales forecasting tool that uses historical data to predict future sales. The tool allows businesses

to set goals, track progress, and make adjustments to their sales strategy as needed.

2. Territory management: Zoho CRM provides a tool for managing sales territories, which helps businesses optimize their sales efforts by assigning leads and accounts to specific sales reps based on their location or other criteria.

3. Sales analytics: Zoho CRM provides a range of sales analytics tools that allow businesses to track their sales performance over time. These tools can be used to identify trends, measure the effectiveness of marketing campaigns, and make data-driven decisions about sales strategy.

4. Customer analytics: Zoho CRM provides tools for analyzing customer behavior, such as their engagement with emails, website visits, and social media activity. These tools can help businesses identify their most engaged customers, and tailor their marketing and sales efforts accordingly.

Overall, Zoho CRM's reporting and analytics capabilities provide businesses with the tools they need to make data-driven decisions and optimize their sales performance. Whether a business is looking to track their sales pipeline, analyze customer behavior, or forecast future sales, Zoho CRM provides the tools and insights they need to succeed.

B. Zoho Books

1. Features

Zoho Books is a cloud-based accounting software that is designed to help small and medium-sized businesses manage their finances more efficiently. It offers a range of features that are easy to use and customizable, making it a popular choice for businesses of all sizes. In this section, we will discuss some of the key features of Zoho Books.

➢ Invoicing: Zoho Books allows you to create and send professional-looking invoices to your customers in a matter of seconds. You can also set up recurring invoices, automate payment reminders, and accept online payments from your customers.

➢ Expense tracking: You can track your expenses by recording all your purchases and bills in Zoho Books. This helps you keep track of your business expenses, manage your cash flow, and prepare accurate financial reports.

➢ Bank reconciliation: Zoho Books can automatically import your bank transactions and reconcile them with your accounting records. This saves you time and helps you avoid errors that could lead to incorrect financial statements.

➢ Inventory management: If your business sells products, Zoho Books can help you manage your inventory more efficiently.

You can track your stock levels, set up reorder points, and create purchase orders for your suppliers.

➢ Project management: Zoho Books allows you to create projects and track their progress. You can assign tasks to your team members, set deadlines, and monitor the time spent on each task. This helps you manage your projects more effectively and ensure that they are completed on time.

➢ Time tracking: If you bill your customers based on the time spent on a project, Zoho Books allows you to track the time spent by you or your team members on each project. You can generate accurate invoices based on the hours worked and ensure that you are paid for all the work you have done.

➢ Reporting: Zoho Books provides a range of financial reports, including balance sheets, profit and loss statements, cash flow statements, and more. You can also create custom reports based on your specific requirements.

➤ Integrations: Zoho Books integrates with a range of third-party apps, including payment gateways, e-commerce platforms, and CRM systems. This allows you to streamline your business processes and automate your workflows.

➤ Multi-currency support: If your business operates in multiple currencies, Zoho Books allows you to create invoices, receive payments, and generate financial reports in different currencies. This makes it easier to manage your finances across different countries and regions.

➤ Mobile app: Zoho Books has a mobile app that allows you to manage your finances on the go. You can create invoices, record expenses, and view financial reports from your smartphone or tablet.

Overall, Zoho Books offers a range of features that can help you manage your finances more efficiently. Whether you are looking to streamline your invoicing, track your expenses, manage your inventory, or track your time, Zoho Books has something to offer. Its customizable interface and easy-to-use features make it a popular choice for small and medium-sized businesses looking for an affordable and reliable accounting solution.

2. Setup and Configuration

Zoho Books is a cloud-based accounting software designed to help businesses manage their finances effectively. It offers a range of features such as invoicing, expense tracking, inventory management, bank reconciliation, and financial reporting, among others. In this section, we will discuss the setup and configuration of Zoho Books, step by step.

Step 1: Sign up for a Zoho Books account

To get started with Zoho Books, you need to sign up for an account on the Zoho Books website. You can do this by going to https://www.zoho.com/books/ and clicking on the 'Sign Up for Free' button. Follow the instructions to create your account.

Step 2: Add your company details

After creating your account, you will be prompted to add your company details. This includes your company name, address, logo, and other relevant information. This information will be used to customize your invoices and other financial documents.

Step 3: Set up your chart of accounts

Your chart of accounts is a list of all the accounts you use to track your business transactions. Zoho Books allows you to customize your chart of accounts to suit your business needs. You can add new accounts, edit existing accounts, and delete accounts that are no longer required.

Step 4: Connect your bank accounts

Zoho Books allows you to connect your bank accounts and credit cards to import transactions automatically. This saves you time and eliminates the need for manual data entry. To connect your bank accounts, go to the 'Banking' section of Zoho Books and follow the instructions.

Step 5: Set up your taxes

If your business is required to collect sales tax or VAT, you need to set up your tax rates in Zoho Books. This includes adding your tax rates, tax agencies, and tax accounts. You can also set up tax rules that apply to specific products or services.

Step 6: Customize your invoices

Zoho Books allows you to customize your invoices to match your brand and style. You can add your logo, change the colors, and include custom fields to capture additional information. You can also set up automatic payment reminders and thank-you messages.

Step 7: Set up your payment gateway

Zoho Books integrates with several payment gateways, including PayPal, Stripe, and Authorize.net. This allows you to accept online payments directly from your invoices. To set up your payment gateway, go to the 'Settings' section of Zoho Books and follow the instructions.

Step 8: Invite your team members

If you have a team, you can invite them to collaborate with you on Zoho Books. You can set up different levels of access for each user, depending on their role in your business. This allows your team to work together on financial tasks and collaborate on projects.

Step 9: Generate reports

Zoho Books offers a range of reports that help you understand your business finances. These include balance sheets, profit and loss statements, cash flow statements, and more. You can customize these reports to show the information you need and export them in various formats.

Step 10: Automate your workflows

Zoho Books allows you to automate your workflows to save time and reduce errors. You can set up workflows for tasks such as invoicing, expense approvals, and payment reminders. This ensures that your financial processes are streamlined and efficient.

Overall, setting up and configuring Zoho Books is a straightforward process. By following the steps above, you can customize Zoho Books to suit your business needs and manage your finances effectively.

3. Managing Invoices and Expenses

Zoho Books is a cloud-based accounting software that enables businesses to manage their finances, including invoices and expenses, with ease. In this section, we will discuss how to manage invoices and expenses with Zoho Books.

Creating Invoices:

To create an invoice, log in to your Zoho Books account and navigate to the Invoices tab. Click on the 'New Invoice' button to create a new invoice. You will need to fill out the necessary information, such as the customer's name, address, and contact information, as well as the product or service provided, quantity, and price. You can also add discounts, taxes, and shipping charges if necessary. Once you have filled out all the necessary information, click 'Save' to create the invoice.

Sending Invoices:

Once you have created an invoice, you can send it to your customer via email. Zoho Books provides you with a customizable email template that you can use to send the invoice to your customer. You can also set up automatic reminders to remind your customers about upcoming or overdue payments.

Tracking Invoices:

Zoho Books allows you to track the status of your invoices. You can see which invoices have been paid, which are overdue, and which are pending. This helps you to keep track of your cash flow and ensure that you are getting paid on time.

Managing Expenses:

Zoho Books also allows you to manage your expenses. You can create an expense by navigating to the Expenses tab and clicking on the 'New Expense' button. You will need to fill out the necessary information, such as the vendor's name, date of the expense, amount, and category. You can also attach receipts or bills to the expense.

Tracking Expenses:

Once you have created an expense, you can track it by navigating to the Expenses tab. Zoho Books provides you with a dashboard that shows you a summary of your expenses, including the total amount spent, the top categories, and the vendors you have paid.

Managing Bank Accounts:

Zoho Books allows you to connect your bank accounts and credit cards to your account. This enables you to automatically import transactions and reconcile them with your invoices and expenses. You can also create bank deposits and withdrawals, as well as transfer funds between accounts.

Generating Reports:

Zoho Books provides you with a variety of reports that help you to understand your financial situation. You can generate reports such as profit and loss, balance sheet, and cash flow statement. You can also customize these reports to suit your needs.

Overall, Zoho Books is a powerful accounting software that enables businesses to manage their finances effectively. With features such as invoicing, expense management, bank account management, and reporting, Zoho Books provides businesses with all the tools they need to manage their finances. By using Zoho Books to manage your invoices and expenses, you can save time, reduce errors, and ensure that your finances are in order.

4. Inventory Management

Inventory management is an essential aspect of any business, and it involves keeping track of the products or goods that a business buys, sells, or produces. Efficient inventory management ensures that businesses always have the right amount of inventory on hand to meet customer demands, reduce waste and spoilage, and optimize profits.

Zoho Books is a cloud-based accounting software that offers an inventory management module to help businesses track their inventory efficiently. The inventory module in Zoho Books allows users to manage their stock levels, track their inventory movements, and automate their inventory-related tasks.

In this section, we will discuss extensively on inventory management with Zoho Books and how it can help businesses optimize their inventory management process.

Inventory Setup

The first step to managing inventory in Zoho Books is to set up your inventory. This involves creating a list of your products or services and adding their respective prices, descriptions, and SKU (Stock Keeping Units) numbers. Zoho Books also allows you to create different product categories and subcategories to organize your inventory.

Inventory Tracking

After setting up your inventory, you can start tracking your inventory movements in Zoho Books. You can do this by recording all the stock that comes in and goes out of your business. Zoho Books allows you to record stock movements manually or by importing data from your suppliers or vendors.

Stock Adjustments

In some cases, your inventory levels may be inaccurate due to loss, damage, or theft. Zoho Books allows you to adjust your stock levels to reflect these changes. You can do this by creating a stock adjustment entry in Zoho Books, which will adjust your inventory levels accordingly.

Purchase Orders

When it's time to restock your inventory, you can create purchase orders in Zoho Books. A purchase order is a document that lists the items you want to purchase from your suppliers or vendors. With Zoho Books, you can create purchase orders, send them to your suppliers or vendors, and track their delivery and payment status.

Sales Orders

When you sell products or services to customers, you can create sales orders in Zoho Books. A sales order is a document that lists the items your customers want to purchase from your business. Zoho Books allows you to create sales orders, track their status, and convert them into invoices when the sale is completed.

Stock Alerts

Zoho Books can help you avoid stockouts or overstocking by setting up stock alerts. Stock alerts notify you when your inventory levels fall below or exceed a specific threshold. This allows you to restock your inventory on time or reduce your stock levels to avoid spoilage or waste.

Reports

Zoho Books provides several inventory-related reports to help you make informed business decisions. Some of the inventory reports available in Zoho Books include stock summary, stock movement, purchase history, sales history, and inventory valuation reports. These reports provide insights into your inventory performance, trends, and profitability.

Overall, Zoho Books offers an efficient and user-friendly inventory management module that helps businesses manage their inventory effectively. With Zoho Books, businesses can track their inventory movements, create purchase and sales orders, adjust their stock levels, set up stock alerts, and generate inventory reports. Zoho Books is an all-in-one solution for small and medium-sized businesses that want to optimize their inventory management process.

5. Reports and Analytics

Zoho Books is a cloud-based accounting software that helps businesses manage their finances and automate their accounting tasks. One of the key features of Zoho Books is its reporting and analytics capabilities, which provide businesses with insights into their financial performance and help them make informed decisions.

Reports in Zoho Books:

Zoho Books offers a wide range of pre-built reports that businesses can use to analyze their financial data. These reports can be accessed through the Reports tab on the dashboard and can be customized to suit specific business needs.

Some of the pre-built reports in Zoho Books include:

- Profit and Loss statement: This report shows a business's revenue, expenses, and net income or loss for a specific period.

- Balance Sheet: This report provides an overview of a business's assets, liabilities, and equity as of a specific date.
- Cash Flow statement: This report shows the inflows and outflows of cash for a specific period, providing insights into a business's liquidity.
- Sales reports: These reports provide insights into a business's sales performance, including sales by product or service, customer, and region.
- Purchase reports: These reports provide insights into a business's purchasing activity, including purchases by vendor and category.

Analytics in Zoho Books:

Zoho Books also offers powerful analytics tools that enable businesses to analyze their financial data in real-time. These tools provide insights into a business's financial performance, enabling them to identify trends and opportunities for growth.

Some of the key analytics features in Zoho Books include:

- Dashboard: The dashboard provides an overview of a business's financial performance, including revenue, expenses, cash flow, and profit and loss.
- Custom reports: Businesses can create custom reports using Zoho Books' drag-and-drop report builder, allowing them to analyze their financial data in the way that best suits their needs.
- Budgeting and forecasting: Zoho Books enables businesses to create budgets and forecasts, which can be compared against actual financial data to identify variances and make informed decisions.
- Project profitability: Zoho Books offers a project profitability report, which enables businesses to analyze the profitability of individual projects and make decisions about future projects.

Benefits of Reports and Analytics in Zoho Books:

The reporting and analytics capabilities in Zoho Books offer several benefits for businesses, including:

1. Improved visibility: Reports and analytics provide businesses with a comprehensive view of their financial performance, enabling them to identify areas for improvement and make informed decisions.
2. Time savings: By automating financial reporting and analysis, businesses can save time and reduce the risk of errors.
3. Data-driven decision making: By analyzing financial data in real-time, businesses can make data-driven decisions about their operations and growth strategies.
4. Improved collaboration: Zoho Books enables businesses to share reports and data with stakeholders, improving collaboration and communication across the organization.

Overall, reports and analytics are essential tools for businesses looking to improve their financial performance and make informed decisions. With its powerful reporting and analytics capabilities,

Zoho Books offers businesses a comprehensive solution for managing their finances and gaining insights into their operations.

C. Zoho Inventory

1. Features

Zoho Inventory is an inventory management software that is designed to help businesses of all sizes manage their inventory levels, sales, and purchases. The software provides a comprehensive suite of tools for businesses to manage their inventory, orders, invoices, and payments. Here are some of the key features of Zoho Inventory:

➤ Inventory Management: Zoho Inventory provides a central location for businesses to manage their inventory. The software enables businesses to track inventory levels in real-time, set reorder points, and generate reports on inventory levels and stock movements.

➢ Order Management: With Zoho Inventory, businesses can create sales orders, purchase orders, and invoices, and track the progress of these orders from creation to fulfillment. The software enables businesses to manage their orders from a single dashboard, providing visibility into the entire order lifecycle.

➢ Barcode Scanning: Zoho Inventory supports barcode scanning, which makes it easy for businesses to manage their inventory levels and track stock movements. The software allows businesses to create and print barcode labels and scan them to update inventory levels.

➢ Multi-Channel Sales: Zoho Inventory integrates with various sales channels, including Amazon, eBay, Etsy, and Shopify. This integration allows businesses to manage their sales and inventory levels across multiple channels from a single dashboard.

➢ Shipping Integration: Zoho Inventory integrates with popular shipping providers such as UPS, FedEx, and USPS, allowing businesses to manage their shipping and fulfillment processes from within the software.

➢ Payment Integration: Zoho Inventory supports payment integration with various payment gateways such as PayPal, Stripe, and Authorize.net, enabling businesses to process payments online.

➢ Reports: Zoho Inventory provides a suite of reports that help businesses gain insights into their inventory levels, sales, purchases, and financial performance. The software enables businesses to generate reports on demand or schedule them to be sent automatically.

➢ Mobile App: Zoho Inventory has a mobile app that allows businesses to manage their inventory and orders on the go. The app provides real-time updates on inventory levels, order status, and sales performance.

➢ Customization: Zoho Inventory allows businesses to customize their workflows, forms, and reports to meet their unique business needs. The software also provides customization options for labels, templates, and branding.

➢ Collaboration: Zoho Inventory enables collaboration among team members, allowing businesses to assign roles and permissions, share documents, and communicate within the software.

Overall, Zoho Inventory provides a robust suite of features that help businesses manage their inventory, orders, and payments more efficiently. The software is designed to be user-friendly and customizable, making it an excellent choice for businesses of all sizes.

2. Setup and Configuration

Zoho Inventory is a cloud-based inventory management software that helps businesses manage their inventory, sales, and purchase orders. It is an efficient tool that allows you to manage your inventory across multiple warehouses and sales channels. The software is easy to set up and configure, and this guide will help you through the process.

1. Sign up for Zoho Inventory

The first step is to sign up for Zoho Inventory. You can sign up for a free trial or subscribe to a paid plan. You will need to provide your business details, including your company name, address, and contact information. Once you have signed up, you will receive an email with your login details.

2. Add your products and services

The next step is to add your products and services to Zoho Inventory. You can do this manually or import them from a CSV file. When adding products, you need to provide details such as the product name, SKU, description, and price.

3. Set up your warehouse

Zoho Inventory allows you to set up multiple warehouses, and you can specify the location, capacity, and address of each warehouse. This feature is particularly useful if you have inventory stored in different locations.

4. Connect your sales channels

Zoho Inventory integrates with various sales channels, including Amazon, eBay, Etsy, and Shopify. You can connect your sales channels to Zoho Inventory, and it will automatically sync your sales orders and inventory levels.

5. Set up your payment gateway

Zoho Inventory also integrates with payment gateways such as PayPal, Stripe, and Square. You can set up your payment gateway in Zoho

Inventory, and it will automatically process your customer payments.

6. Configure your taxes

You can configure your taxes in Zoho Inventory based on your business location and the locations of your customers. You can set up multiple tax rates for different products and services.

7. Set up your users and roles

Zoho Inventory allows you to set up multiple users with different roles and permissions. You can set up user accounts for your employees, and you can specify the level of access each user has.

8. Customize your settings

Zoho Inventory allows you to customize various settings, including your invoice and order templates, email notifications, and currency settings. You can also set up custom fields to track additional information about your products and services.

3. Managing Orders and Fulfillment

Zoho Inventory is a cloud-based inventory management software that helps businesses to manage their orders, inventory, and fulfillment process. With Zoho Inventory, you can easily create and manage orders, track your inventory levels, and automate your fulfillment process. In this section, we will discuss how to manage orders and fulfillment with Zoho Inventory.

Creating Orders:

To create an order in Zoho Inventory, you can navigate to the "Orders" tab and click on the "Create Order" button. You will then be prompted to enter the customer information, product details, and shipping information. You can also add any notes or attachments to the order. Once you have entered all the necessary information, you can save the order.

Managing Orders:

Zoho Inventory allows you to easily manage your orders. You can view all your orders in the "Orders" tab and filter them by status, date, or customer. You can also edit, delete, or duplicate orders if needed. Zoho Inventory also allows you to print packing slips and invoices for your orders.

Fulfillment:

Zoho Inventory offers various options for fulfilling your orders. You can fulfill orders manually, by marking them as "Fulfilled" in the order details page. You can also use Zoho Inventory's integration with shipping carriers to generate shipping labels and track shipments. You can also set up automated workflows to streamline your fulfillment process.

Inventory Management:

Zoho Inventory helps you keep track of your inventory levels in real-time. When you create an order, Zoho Inventory automatically updates your inventory levels, so you always know what you have in stock. You can also set up low stock alerts to notify you when inventory levels are running low.

Integration:

Zoho Inventory integrates with various e-commerce platforms, such as Shopify and WooCommerce, to automatically sync your orders and inventory levels. Zoho Inventory also integrates with shipping carriers, such as FedEx and UPS, to generate shipping labels and track shipments. Additionally, Zoho Inventory integrates with accounting software, such as Zoho Books and QuickBooks, to automate your accounting processes.

Overall, Zoho Inventory is a powerful inventory management software that can help you manage your orders and fulfillment process. By using Zoho Inventory, you can streamline your operations, save time, and improve your customer experience.

4. Stock Management

Zoho Inventory is a cloud-based inventory management system that helps businesses streamline their stock management processes. This software allows businesses to track inventory levels, monitor stock movements, and automate the order fulfillment process. In this section, we will discuss the key features of Zoho Inventory and how they can help businesses manage their stocks effectively.

1. Inventory Tracking

Zoho Inventory allows businesses to track their inventory levels in real-time. This means that they can monitor their stock levels at any time, from any location. The software provides businesses with a detailed overview of their stock levels, including the quantity on hand, on order, and in transit. This information can help businesses make informed decisions about when to reorder products and how much to order.

2. Order Management

Zoho Inventory helps businesses automate their order fulfillment process. The software allows businesses to create and manage sales orders, purchase orders, and invoices. It also enables businesses to track the status of their orders and monitor their fulfillment progress. This feature helps businesses ensure that their customers receive their orders on time and in full.

3. Multi-channel Selling

Zoho Inventory integrates with multiple sales channels, including Amazon, eBay, and Shopify. This integration allows businesses to manage their sales and inventory across multiple channels from a single platform. It also enables businesses to sync their inventory levels across all channels, reducing the risk of overselling or underselling.

4. Barcode Scanning

Zoho Inventory supports barcode scanning, making it easy for businesses to manage their stock movements. This feature allows businesses to scan items as they enter or leave the warehouse, updating their inventory levels in real-time. It also enables businesses to track the movement of their stock from one location to another.

5. Reporting and Analytics

Zoho Inventory provides businesses with detailed reports and analytics, helping them make data-driven decisions. The software provides businesses with insights into their inventory levels, order status, and sales performance. This information can help businesses identify trends and make informed decisions about their stock management processes.

6. Integrations

Zoho Inventory integrates with a range of third-party apps, including accounting software, shipping carriers, and payment gateways. This integration allows businesses to streamline their stock management processes and reduce manual data entry.

Overall, Zoho Inventory is a powerful inventory management system that can help businesses manage their stocks effectively. The software provides businesses with a range of features, including inventory tracking, order management, multi-channel selling, barcode scanning, reporting and analytics, and integrations. These features can help businesses streamline their stock management processes, reduce manual data entry, and make informed decisions about their inventory levels.

5. Reports and Analytics

Zoho Inventory is a powerful inventory management software that offers a range of tools for businesses to manage their inventory, track orders and shipments, and generate reports and analytics. With Zoho Inventory, businesses can gain insights into their sales, inventory, and customer behavior, and make informed decisions to optimize their operations and boost profitability.

Reports and analytics are a key feature of Zoho Inventory, allowing businesses to generate detailed reports on various aspects of their inventory and sales. These reports provide valuable insights into the performance of the business, highlighting areas of strength and weakness and identifying opportunities for improvement.

Some of the key reports and analytics features of Zoho Inventory include:

1. Sales Reports: Zoho Inventory offers a range of sales reports, including sales summary reports, sales by item reports, sales by customer reports, and sales by location reports. These reports provide a detailed analysis of sales performance, including top-selling products, best-performing customers, and most profitable locations.

2. Inventory Reports: Zoho Inventory offers a range of inventory reports, including inventory summary reports, inventory valuation reports, and inventory aging reports. These reports provide a detailed analysis of inventory levels, value, and age, allowing businesses to optimize their inventory management and avoid stockouts and overstocking.

3. Purchase Reports: Zoho Inventory offers a range of purchase reports, including purchase order reports, purchase history reports, and purchase by vendor reports. These reports provide a detailed analysis of purchase performance, including top vendors, most purchased items, and purchase history.

4. Financial Reports: Zoho Inventory offers a range of financial reports, including profit and loss reports, balance sheet reports, and cash flow reports. These reports provide a detailed analysis of the financial performance of the business, including revenue, expenses, assets, liabilities, and cash flow.

5. Customer Reports: Zoho Inventory offers a range of customer reports, including customer history reports, customer sales reports, and customer aging reports. These reports provide a detailed analysis of customer behavior, including purchase history, top-selling products, and outstanding balances.

In addition to these standard reports, Zoho Inventory also offers customizable reports, allowing businesses to create their own reports based on their unique needs and requirements. With customizable reports, businesses can generate tailored reports that provide insights into specific aspects of their operations, allowing them to make informed decisions and optimize their performance.

Overall, Zoho Inventory offers a comprehensive set of reports and analytics features that allow businesses to gain valuable insights into their operations and make informed decisions to optimize their performance. With detailed reports on sales, inventory, purchases, finance, and customers, businesses can identify areas of strength and weakness, optimize their inventory management, and boost profitability.

D. Zoho Desk

1. Features

Zoho Desk is a cloud-based help desk software that offers a comprehensive set of features to help businesses manage customer support tickets and inquiries effectively. This software can be used by small to medium-sized businesses as well as large enterprises that require an efficient and scalable help desk solution. Some of the key features of Zoho Desk are:

> Ticket Management: Zoho Desk allows businesses to manage all customer support tickets in one place. Agents can create, assign, and track tickets from multiple channels such as email, social media, phone, and chat. The software also enables agents to set priorities and due dates for tickets, ensuring that they are resolved within the designated time.

> Multi-Channel Support: Zoho Desk allows businesses to provide support across

multiple channels, including email, social media, chat, and phone. This feature enables businesses to engage with customers on the channels they prefer, improving customer satisfaction and loyalty.

➢ Automation: Zoho Desk comes with a range of automation tools that help businesses streamline their support processes. For instance, the software can automatically assign tickets to the right agent based on their expertise or workload. It can also send automated responses to customers, notifying them of ticket updates or closures.

➢ Collaboration: Zoho Desk enables agents to collaborate on tickets, allowing them to share information, assign tasks, and escalate issues to other teams. This feature ensures that tickets are resolved faster and more efficiently, improving customer satisfaction.

➢ Analytics and Reporting: Zoho Desk provides businesses with detailed analytics and reporting tools, allowing them to track key metrics such as ticket volume, response time, and customer satisfaction. The software can generate custom reports that help businesses identify areas for improvement and optimize their support processes.

- ➢ Self-Service: Zoho Desk offers a self-service portal that enables customers to find answers to their questions without contacting support. Businesses can create a knowledge base of articles, FAQs, and tutorials that customers can access at any time. This feature reduces the workload on agents and improves customer satisfaction.

- ➢ Integrations: Zoho Desk integrates with a range of third-party applications such as CRM, project management, and collaboration tools. This feature enables businesses to streamline their workflows and improve productivity.

Overall, Zoho Desk offers a comprehensive set of features that help businesses manage customer support tickets and inquiries effectively. The software's multi-channel support, automation, collaboration, analytics, and reporting tools, self-service portal, and integrations make it a powerful and scalable help desk solution for businesses of all sizes.

2. Setup and Configuration

Zoho Desk is a cloud-based customer service and support software that helps businesses manage and resolve customer issues efficiently. To get started with Zoho Desk, you need to set up and configure your account, which involves several steps.

1. Sign Up for Zoho Desk

To start using Zoho Desk, you need to sign up for an account. Go to the Zoho Desk website and click the "Sign Up for Free" button. You will be asked to provide your company name, email address, and phone number. Once you have filled in the required details, click the "Sign Up" button.

2. Add Users and Set up Roles

After signing up, you can add users to your Zoho Desk account. You can add agents, managers, and administrators. To add a user, click on the "Settings" icon and select "Users & Roles." Click on the "Add User" button and enter the user's details, including their name and email address. You can also assign a role to the user, such as agent or manager.

3. Configure Email

Zoho Desk allows you to receive and respond to customer emails from within the software. To configure your email, go to the "Settings" icon and select "Email." Click on the "Add Email Account" button and enter your email address and password. You can also configure your email settings to customize how you receive and send emails.

4. Set up Ticket Fields

Ticket fields help you organize and prioritize customer issues. You can create custom ticket fields to capture specific information about a customer's issue. To set up ticket fields, go to the "Settings" icon and select "Fields." Click on the "Add Field" button and select the type of field you want to create. You can choose from options such as text, dropdown, and checkbox.

5. Create Help Center

Zoho Desk allows you to create a help center where customers can find answers to frequently asked questions. To create a help center, go to the "Settings" icon and select "Help Center." Click on the "Create a New Portal" button and enter the details for your help center, such as the name and URL. You can also customize the look and feel of your help center.

6. Set up Automation

Zoho Desk provides automation features that help you streamline your support processes. You can set up automation rules to automatically assign tickets to agents, send notifications, and perform other actions based on predefined criteria. To set up automation rules, go to the "Settings" icon and select "Automation." Click on the "Add Rule" button and configure the rule based on your requirements.

7. Integrate with Other Apps

Zoho Desk integrates with other apps such as Zoho CRM, Google Analytics, and Slack. Integration allows you to share data between apps and streamline your workflow. To integrate with other apps, go to the "Settings" icon and select "Integrations." Click on the app you want to integrate with and follow the instructions.

Overall, setting up and configuring Zoho Desk involves several steps, including adding users, configuring email, setting up ticket fields, creating a help center, setting up automation, and integrating with other apps. By following these steps, you can create a customized support system that meets your business needs.

3. Managing Support Tickets

Zoho Desk is a powerful and versatile customer support software that allows businesses to efficiently manage their customer support tickets. Support tickets can be created by customers through various channels, such as email, phone, social media, chat, and more. Zoho Desk brings all of these channels together into a single platform, allowing businesses to track and manage their support tickets in a centralized location. In this section, we will discuss how to manage support tickets with Zoho Desk.

- **Set Up Your Help Desk**

Before you can start managing your support tickets, you need to set up your help desk in Zoho Desk. This involves configuring your support channels, such as email, social media, and chat, and setting up your ticketing system. Zoho Desk makes it easy to set up your help desk with its intuitive interface and step-by-step guides.

- **Create Ticket Categories**

To help you organize and prioritize your support tickets, Zoho Desk allows you to create ticket categories. These categories can be based on the type of issue or the product or service that the customer is using. By categorizing your tickets, you can quickly identify the most urgent issues and assign them to the appropriate team members.

- **Assign Tickets to Agents**

Zoho Desk allows you to assign support tickets to individual agents or teams based on their expertise and workload. This helps ensure that each ticket is handled by the most qualified and available agent. You can also set up rules to automatically assign tickets based on their category, priority, or other criteria.

- **Set Up SLAs**

Service level agreements (SLAs) are agreements between businesses and their customers that define the expected response and resolution times for support tickets. Zoho Desk allows you to set up

SLAs for your support tickets, which helps ensure that you meet your customers' expectations. You can set up SLAs based on ticket priority, category, and other criteria.

- **Monitor Ticket Progress**

Zoho Desk provides real-time updates on the progress of each support ticket. You can monitor the status of each ticket, view the agent's notes and comments, and see the entire ticket history. This helps you stay informed about the progress of each ticket and ensure that your agents are providing high-quality support.

- **Automate Your Workflow**

Zoho Desk offers a range of automation features that can help you streamline your support ticket management workflow. For example, you can set up rules to automatically assign tickets to specific agents, send automated responses to customers, and escalate tickets that have not been resolved within a certain timeframe.

- **Analyze Your Data**

Zoho Desk provides detailed reports and analytics on your support ticket data. You can analyze data such as ticket volume, response times, resolution times, and customer satisfaction scores. This helps you identify areas where you can improve your support processes and ensure that your customers are satisfied with your service.

Overall, Zoho Desk is a powerful customer support software that allows businesses to efficiently manage their support tickets. By following the tips outlined above, businesses can use Zoho Desk to organize, prioritize, and resolve their support tickets in a timely and effective manner. With Zoho Desk, businesses can provide high-quality support to their customers and build strong, long-lasting relationships.

4. Knowledge Base

Zoho Desk is a cloud-based helpdesk software that provides businesses with a comprehensive customer support solution. One of the key features of Zoho Desk is its knowledge base, which enables businesses to create and maintain a repository of information that customers can access to find answers to their questions.

The knowledge base in Zoho Desk is a centralized location where businesses can store all their support articles, FAQs, and other types of customer-facing content. It is a self-service platform that allows customers to find the information they need without having to reach out to a support agent. This not only helps to reduce the workload on support staff but also improves customer satisfaction by providing quick and accurate solutions.

With Zoho Desk's knowledge base, businesses can create articles and organize them into categories and subcategories. Articles can be created in multiple languages, and businesses can use tags to make them easy to find. The knowledge base can also be customized with the company's branding and can be integrated with the business's website.

One of the key advantages of using Zoho Desk's knowledge base is that it can help businesses to reduce support costs. By providing customers with a self-service platform, businesses can reduce the number of support tickets they receive and save on support staff salaries. Additionally, the knowledge base can help businesses to improve their support team's efficiency by reducing the time it takes to resolve support requests.

Zoho Desk's knowledge base also includes analytics that businesses can use to track the performance of their articles. The analytics provide insights into how many views each article receives, which articles are most popular, and which articles need to be improved. This can help businesses to refine their content and improve the overall quality of their knowledge base.

Another advantage of using Zoho Desk's knowledge base is that it can help businesses to improve their SEO. By optimizing their articles with relevant keywords, businesses can increase their visibility in search engines and drive more traffic to their website. This can help to attract new customers and improve customer retention.

Overall, Zoho Desk's knowledge base is a powerful tool that can help businesses to provide better customer support, reduce support costs, and improve customer satisfaction. By creating a centralized repository of information that customers can access at any time, businesses can provide quick and accurate solutions to their customers' problems. The analytics and customization options also make it easy for businesses to refine their content and improve their support processes over time.

5. Reports and Analytics

Zoho Desk is a powerful help desk software that helps businesses manage their customer support operations efficiently. One of the key features of Zoho Desk is its robust reporting and analytics capabilities, which allow businesses to gain insights into their support operations and make data-driven decisions. In this section, we will explore the various reports and analytics features offered by Zoho Desk and how businesses can use them to improve their customer support operations.

Reports in Zoho Desk

Zoho Desk offers a wide range of reports that can help businesses track various metrics related to their support operations. These reports can be accessed from the Reports tab in the Zoho Desk dashboard. Let's take a look at some of the key reports offered by Zoho Desk:

> ➤ Ticket Reports: Ticket reports allow businesses to track the number of tickets raised, resolved, and pending. These reports can be used to identify trends and patterns in

ticket volumes, and help businesses optimize their support operations accordingly.

➤ SLA Reports: SLA reports help businesses track their adherence to service level agreements (SLAs). Businesses can track metrics such as first response time, resolution time, and overall SLA compliance. This information can be used to identify areas for improvement and optimize support operations.

➤ Customer Reports: Customer reports allow businesses to track customer satisfaction ratings, feedback, and other metrics related to customer interactions. This information can be used to identify areas for improvement in customer support and tailor support operations to better meet customer needs.

➤ Agent Reports: Agent reports allow businesses to track agent performance metrics such as ticket resolution rates, response times, and customer satisfaction ratings. This information can be used to identify high-performing agents, provide targeted training to underperforming agents, and optimize overall agent performance.

➢ Custom Reports: Zoho Desk also allows businesses to create custom reports based on their unique needs. Businesses can choose from a range of metrics and filters to create custom reports that provide insights into their support operations.

Analytics in Zoho Desk

In addition to reports, Zoho Desk also offers a range of analytics features that allow businesses to gain deeper insights into their support operations. Let's take a look at some of the key analytics features offered by Zoho Desk:

➢ AI-Powered Analytics: Zoho Desk's AI-powered analytics feature uses machine learning algorithms to analyze support data and provide insights into customer behavior, agent performance, and other key metrics.

This feature can help businesses identify trends and patterns that may not be immediately apparent in traditional reports.

➢ Dashboard Customization: Zoho Desk allows businesses to customize their dashboard to display the metrics and reports that are most relevant to their business. This can help businesses stay focused on their key performance indicators and make data-driven decisions.

➢ Real-Time Analytics: Zoho Desk provides real-time analytics that allow businesses to track support metrics as they happen. This can be particularly useful in high-volume support environments where quick decision-making is critical.

➢ Social Media Analytics: Zoho Desk also offers social media analytics that allow businesses to track their social media presence and engagement with customers.

This can help businesses identify opportunities to improve their social media strategy and better engage with their customers.

Overall, Zoho Desk's reports and analytics features provide businesses with a wealth of information about their support operations. By tracking metrics related to ticket volumes, agent performance, customer satisfaction, and other key areas, businesses can identify areas for improvement and optimize their support operations accordingly. With AI-powered analytics, real-time metrics, and social media analytics, Zoho Desk provides businesses with the tools they need to make data-driven decisions and provide exceptional customer support.

E. Zoho Projects

1. Features

Zoho Projects is a cloud-based project management software that helps teams to plan, track, and collaborate on projects from start to finish. It offers a wide range of features that help teams to manage tasks, resources, and timelines efficiently. Here are some of the key features of Zoho Projects:

- ➤ Project Planning: With Zoho Projects, you can plan your projects using Gantt charts, Kanban boards, and task lists. This feature allows you to assign tasks to team members, set deadlines, and prioritize tasks based on their importance.

- ➤ Time Tracking: Zoho Projects provides a built-in time tracker that allows team members to log the time spent on tasks. This feature helps project managers to monitor the progress of a project in real-time and adjust schedules accordingly.

➢ Resource Management: Zoho Projects allows you to manage resources such as team members, equipment, and materials. You can assign resources to tasks and monitor their availability to ensure that they are used efficiently.

➢ Collaboration: Zoho Projects provides a collaborative environment where team members can share files, comments, and feedback. This feature helps to streamline communication and ensures that everyone is on the same page.

➢ Reporting: Zoho Projects provides a wide range of reports that allow you to monitor project progress, resource utilization, and team performance. You can export these reports in various formats such as Excel, PDF, and CSV.

➢ Budgeting: Zoho Projects allows you to set budgets for projects and monitor expenses in real-time. This feature helps to ensure that projects are completed within budget.

➢ Customization: Zoho Projects provides a high degree of customization that allows you to tailor the software to meet the specific needs of your organization. You can customize workflows, fields, and dashboards to match your requirements.

➢ Integrations: Zoho Projects integrates with a wide range of third-party apps such as Google Drive, Dropbox, and Slack. This feature allows you to centralize your work and streamline your workflow.

➢ Mobile App: Zoho Projects provides a mobile app that allows team members to access project information from anywhere. The app is available on both iOS and Android devices.

Overall, Zoho Projects offers a comprehensive set of features that help teams to manage projects efficiently. From project planning to reporting, Zoho Projects provides a range of tools that enable teams to collaborate effectively and deliver projects on time and within budget.

2. Setup and Configuration

Zoho Projects is a comprehensive project management tool that helps businesses plan and manage their projects efficiently. The setup and configuration process of Zoho Projects is straightforward and can be done by following a few simple steps. In this section, I will walk you through the setup and configuration process of Zoho Projects.

1. Create a Zoho Projects Account

The first step in setting up Zoho Projects is to create a Zoho account. To create a Zoho account, go to the Zoho Projects website and click on the "Sign Up for Free" button. You will then be prompted to enter your name, email address, and a password. After filling in the required details, click on the "Sign Up" button to create your Zoho account.

2. Create a New Project

Once you have created a Zoho account, the next step is to create a new project. To create a new project, log in to your Zoho Projects account and click on the "Create Project" button. You will then be prompted to enter the name of the project, the project manager's name, the start and end dates of the project, and other relevant details. Once you have filled in the required details, click on the "Create Project" button to create a new project.

3. Customize Your Project

After creating a new project, the next step is to customize your project according to your requirements. To customize your project, click on the "Settings" icon located in the top right corner of the project dashboard. From the settings menu, you can customize various aspects of your project, such as project templates, project milestones, task lists, and project status.

4. Invite Team Members

Once you have customized your project, the next step is to invite team members to collaborate on the project. To invite team members, click on the "Team" tab located in the top menu bar of the project dashboard. From the team tab, you can invite team members by entering their email addresses or by importing them from a CSV file.

5. Configure User Roles and Permissions

After inviting team members, the next step is to configure user roles and permissions. User roles and permissions enable you to control the access and functionality available to each team member. To configure user roles and permissions, click on the "Roles and Permissions" tab located in the "Team" section of the project dashboard. From the roles and permissions tab, you can define user roles, set user permissions, and assign roles to team members.

6. Integrate Third-Party Apps

Zoho Projects integrates seamlessly with various third-party apps, such as Google Drive, Dropbox, and GitHub. To integrate third-party apps, click on the "Integrations" tab located in the top menu bar of the project dashboard. From the integrations tab, you can connect Zoho Projects with various third-party apps by entering your login credentials.

7. Set Up Reports and Dashboards

Zoho Projects offers powerful reporting and analytics tools that enable you to monitor the progress of your project and make data-driven decisions. To set up reports and dashboards, click on the "Reports" tab located in the top menu bar of the project dashboard. From the reports tab, you can create custom reports, set up dashboards, and configure notifications and alerts.

Overall, setting up and configuring Zoho Projects is a straightforward process that can be done by following a few simple steps. By customizing your project, inviting team members, configuring user roles and permissions, integrating third-party apps, and setting up reports and dashboards, you can ensure that your project is managed efficiently and effectively.

3. Managing Tasks and Milestones

Zoho Projects is a powerful project management tool that can help you manage tasks and milestones efficiently. With its intuitive interface and robust features, you can easily create, assign, track, and manage tasks, set deadlines and milestones, and collaborate with your team members in real-time. In this section, we will explore how to manage tasks and milestones with Zoho Projects.

- **Creating Tasks**

The first step to managing tasks in Zoho Projects is to create them. You can create tasks either from scratch or by cloning an existing task. When you create a new task, you can assign it to a team member, set its start and due dates, and add any necessary details or notes.

- **Assigning Tasks**

Once you have created a task, you can assign it to a team member. You can either assign tasks to specific team members or to a group of team members. You can also set the priority of each task to help your team members understand which tasks are most important and require immediate attention.

- **Tracking Tasks**

With Zoho Projects, you can easily track the progress of each task. You can view the status of a task, see when it was last updated, and track its progress towards completion. You can also add comments and notes to a task to keep everyone on the same page.

- **Setting Milestones**

Milestones are important checkpoints in your project timeline that help you track progress and stay on schedule. With Zoho Projects, you can easily set milestones for your project and track progress towards them. You can set milestones for specific dates, such as the completion of a major task or the delivery of a key component of your project.

- **Tracking Milestones**

Once you have set milestones for your project, you can track progress towards them in real-time. You can see which milestones have been achieved and which ones are still outstanding. You can also see the estimated completion dates for each milestone and adjust your project timeline accordingly.

- **Collaborating with Team Members**

With Zoho Projects, you can collaborate with your team members in real-time. You can share files, documents, and other project-related information with your team members. You can also set up discussions and forums to facilitate communication and collaboration among team members.

Overall, Managing tasks and milestones is essential to the success of any project. With Zoho Projects, you can easily create, assign, track, and manage tasks, set milestones, and collaborate with your team members in real-time. By using Zoho Projects to manage your projects, you can streamline your project management process and ensure that your projects are completed on time and within budget.

4. Time Tracking

Zoho Projects is a project management software that allows users to manage their projects efficiently. One of the key features of Zoho Projects is time tracking, which allows users to keep track of the time spent on each task within a project. In this section, we will explore time tracking with Zoho Projects and how it can help users manage their projects effectively.

Setting up Time Tracking in Zoho Projects

To start using time tracking in Zoho Projects, you need to enable the feature first. You can do this by following these steps:

- Log in to your Zoho Projects account.
- Click on the 'Settings' icon on the top right corner of the page.
- In the drop-down menu, select 'General Settings'.
- Scroll down to 'Time Tracking' and toggle the switch to enable it.
- Click on 'Save'.

Once you have enabled time tracking, you can start tracking time for your tasks.

Using Time Tracking in Zoho Projects

To track time for a task in Zoho Projects, you need to follow these steps:

- Navigate to the task you want to track time for.

- Click on the 'Track Time' button located on the top right corner of the page.
- In the pop-up window, enter the start time and end time for the task.
- You can also add any notes or comments related to the task.
- Click on 'Save' to record the time spent on the task.

You can also track time using the Zoho Projects mobile app. To track time using the mobile app, follow these steps:

- Open the Zoho Projects app on your mobile device.
- Navigate to the task you want to track time for.
- Click on the 'Track Time' button located at the bottom of the page.
- Enter the start time and end time for the task.
- You can also add any notes or comments related to the task.
- Click on 'Save' to record the time spent on the task.

Viewing Time Tracking Reports

Zoho Projects provides several reports that allow you to view the time spent on tasks. These reports can help you analyze the time spent on each task and identify areas where you can improve efficiency. To view time tracking reports in Zoho Projects, follow these steps:

- Click on the 'Reports' tab located on the top menu bar of the page.
- Select 'Time Tracking' from the drop-down menu.
- You can choose from several reports such as 'Timesheet', 'Task Time Log', 'Team Utilization', and 'Invoice Report'.
- Each report provides different insights into the time spent on tasks.

Benefits of Time Tracking with Zoho Projects

Time tracking with Zoho Projects offers several benefits, including:

1. Improved Efficiency: Time tracking allows you to identify areas where you are spending too much time and take steps to improve efficiency.

2. Accurate Billing: Time tracking ensures that you bill your clients accurately for the time spent on their projects.

3. Project Monitoring: Time tracking allows you to monitor the progress of your projects and ensure that they are on track.

4. Employee Productivity: Time tracking helps you identify employees who are performing well and those who need additional training.

Overall, Time tracking is an essential feature of project management, and Zoho Projects provides a comprehensive solution for time tracking. By enabling time tracking in Zoho Projects, you can improve efficiency, monitor project progress, and ensure accurate billing. With the help of time tracking reports, you can analyze the time spent on each task and identify areas for improvement.

5. Reports and Analytics

Zoho Projects is a powerful project management software that allows teams to plan, collaborate and execute projects efficiently. One of the key features of Zoho Projects is its reporting and analytics capabilities. These features enable project managers to track project progress, identify potential risks, and make informed decisions based on data.

In this section, we'll explore the various reports and analytics tools available in Zoho Projects and how they can be used to improve project performance.

- **Overview Reports**

Overview reports in Zoho Projects provide a high-level view of project progress. These reports include charts and graphs that display key metrics such as task completion, milestones achieved, and budget utilization. Overview reports can be customized to show information relevant to your project, and they can be exported as PDF or CSV files.

- **Resource Utilization Reports**

Resource utilization reports show how team members are utilizing their time on tasks. These reports can be used to identify potential bottlenecks in the project and allocate resources more effectively. Resource utilization reports can also be used to track billable hours for clients or internal stakeholders.

- **Time Tracking Reports**

Time tracking reports provide a detailed view of how much time team members are spending on each task. This information can be used to identify tasks that are taking longer than expected and to allocate resources more effectively. Time tracking reports can also be used to track billable hours for clients or internal stakeholders.

- **Burndown Charts**

Burndown charts show the progress of a project over time. These charts display how much work has been completed versus how much work remains. Burndown charts are useful for identifying potential delays in the project and for making adjustments to the project plan to stay on track.

- **Gantt Charts**

Gantt charts are a popular project management tool that show the timeline of a project. These charts display tasks as bars on a timeline, allowing project managers to visualize the duration and dependencies of each task. Gantt charts are useful for identifying potential delays and dependencies in the project and for making adjustments to the project plan to stay on track.

- **Custom Reports**

Zoho Projects also allows users to create custom reports that are tailored to their specific project needs. Custom reports can include any combination of data points, charts, and graphs. Custom reports are useful for tracking metrics that are not included in the standard reports provided by Zoho Projects.

In addition to the reporting tools listed above, Zoho Projects also includes powerful analytics tools that provide deeper insights into project performance. These tools include:

1. **Predictive Analytics**

   Zoho Projects uses machine learning algorithms to analyze project data and predict potential risks and delays. These predictions are displayed in a dashboard that provides an at-a-glance view of potential issues that need to be addressed.

2. **Resource Allocation**

   Zoho Projects allows users to allocate resources based on project needs. This feature helps to ensure that team members are working on tasks that are aligned with their skills and availability.

3. **Project Health Check**

   Zoho Projects includes a project health check feature that evaluates the overall health of a project based on key metrics such as task completion, milestones achieved, and budget utilization. This feature provides project managers with a quick way to identify potential issues and make informed decisions based on data.

Overall, Zoho Projects provides a wide range of reporting and analytics tools that can be used to improve project performance. These tools enable project managers to track project progress, identify potential risks, and make informed decisions based on data. Whether you're looking for high-level overview reports or deep insights into project performance, Zoho Projects has the tools you need to succeed.

IV. ADVANCED FEATURES AND CUSTOMIZATIONS

A. Zoho Creator

Zoho Creator is a cloud-based low-code application development platform that allows users to create custom business applications without writing a single line of code. It is a product of Zoho Corporation, a company that offers a suite of cloud-based software applications designed for businesses of all sizes. Zoho Creator enables users to build powerful applications for various purposes, including CRM, project management, inventory management, and more.

Features and Benefits of Zoho Creator

1. Low-code development: Zoho Creator provides a low-code environment that allows users to create applications without extensive coding knowledge. This means that users can create applications using simple drag-and-drop tools, which reduces the time and cost of app development.

2. Customizable templates: Zoho Creator comes with a wide range of customizable templates that can be used to build applications quickly. These templates cover various business functions, including project management, CRM, and inventory management.

3. Integration with other Zoho applications: Zoho Creator integrates with other Zoho applications, such as Zoho CRM, Zoho Books, and Zoho Invoice, allowing users to create a seamless workflow between different business functions.

4. Mobile app support: Zoho Creator provides a mobile app that allows users to access their applications from their smartphones and tablets. The mobile app is available for both iOS and Android platforms.

5. Automated workflows: Zoho Creator allows users to automate various workflows, such as sending emails, updating records, and triggering actions based on specific events.

6. Data management: Zoho Creator provides a robust database management system that allows users to manage their data effectively. Users can create custom reports, import data from various sources, and create dashboards to visualize their data.

7. Security: Zoho Creator provides robust security features, including data encryption, user access control, and role-based permissions.

8. Cost-effective: Zoho Creator offers a cost-effective solution for app development, with a variety of pricing plans available to suit different business needs.

Uses of Zoho Creator

- CRM: Zoho Creator can be used to build custom CRM applications to manage customer relationships, sales, and marketing campaigns.

- Project management: Zoho Creator can be used to build custom project management applications to manage tasks, schedules, and project timelines.

- Inventory management: Zoho Creator can be used to build custom inventory management applications to track inventory levels, reorder stock, and manage suppliers.

- Human resources management: Zoho Creator can be used to build custom HR management applications to manage employee records, recruitment, and training.

- Event management: Zoho Creator can be used to build custom event management applications to manage event registration, ticket sales, and attendee tracking.

Overall, Zoho Creator is a powerful low-code application development platform that enables businesses to create custom applications quickly and easily. With a wide range of customizable templates, integration with other Zoho applications, and robust security features, Zoho Creator is an excellent choice for businesses of all sizes. Whether you need to manage customer relationships, track inventory, or manage HR functions, Zoho Creator provides a cost-effective and efficient solution.

B. Zoho Flow

Zoho Flow is a cloud-based integration platform that allows businesses to automate workflows across multiple applications without the need for coding skills. It enables businesses to integrate data between cloud applications, automate business processes, and streamline workflows. With Zoho Flow, businesses can connect their apps and create powerful workflows that automate repetitive tasks, improving efficiency, productivity, and accuracy.

Zoho Flow is designed to integrate with over 500 popular cloud applications, including Zoho CRM, Salesforce, Shopify, Slack, Trello, Quickbooks, and many more. It supports a wide range of integration types, such as triggers, actions, and searches, making it easy for businesses to create complex workflows that integrate data from multiple applications.

Some of the key features of Zoho Flow include:

1. Workflow automation: Zoho Flow allows businesses to automate repetitive tasks and streamline workflows by creating automated workflows between multiple applications.

2. Customizable workflows: With Zoho Flow, businesses can customize workflows based on their specific needs and requirements.

3. Pre-built templates: Zoho Flow provides pre-built templates for common workflows, such as lead capture, order fulfillment, and invoice creation.

4. Multi-step workflows: Zoho Flow supports multi-step workflows that can integrate data from multiple applications and perform multiple actions.

5. Real-time synchronization: Zoho Flow ensures that data is synchronized in real-time across all integrated applications, ensuring that businesses always have access to up-to-date information.

6. Conditional workflows: Zoho Flow allows businesses to create conditional workflows that trigger specific actions based on predefined conditions.

7. Robust security: Zoho Flow provides robust security features, such as SSL encryption and OAuth authentication, to ensure that data is always secure.

8. User-friendly interface: Zoho Flow has a user-friendly interface that makes it easy for businesses to create, manage, and monitor workflows.

9. Zoho Flow can be used by businesses of all sizes, from small startups to large enterprises. It is particularly useful for businesses that rely on multiple cloud applications and need to integrate data between them. With Zoho Flow, businesses can automate workflows, save time, and reduce the risk of errors that can occur when data is manually transferred between applications.

Overall, Zoho Flow is an excellent tool for businesses that want to streamline workflows and automate repetitive tasks. With its wide range of integration options, pre-built templates, and user-friendly interface, Zoho Flow makes it easy for businesses to create powerful workflows that integrate data from multiple applications.

C. Zoho Campaigns

Zoho Campaigns is a comprehensive email marketing automation tool that allows businesses to create, send, and track email campaigns. It is a product of Zoho Corporation, a leading provider of business software solutions, and is designed to help businesses of all sizes improve their email marketing efforts.

Zoho Campaigns comes with a variety of features that allow businesses to create engaging and personalized email campaigns. The tool provides a drag-and-drop email editor, which makes it easy to create visually appealing emails without the need for coding or design skills. Users can also choose from a variety of pre-built email templates to quickly create professional-looking emails.

The tool also provides several automation features, including workflows and autoresponders, that allow businesses to create targeted and personalized campaigns. With workflows, businesses can set up a series of automated emails that are triggered by specific user actions, such as signing up for a newsletter or making a purchase. Autoresponders, on the other hand, allow businesses to automatically send a welcome email or confirmation email when a user completes a specific action.

Zoho Campaigns also provides advanced list management features, allowing businesses to segment their email list based on various criteria, such as demographics or purchase history. This allows businesses to create highly targeted campaigns that are more likely to convert.

The tool also provides analytics features that allow businesses to track the performance of their email campaigns. Users can track metrics such as open rates, click-through rates, and conversion rates to measure the success of their campaigns. The tool also provides A/B testing features, which allow businesses to test different email variations to see which performs better.

Zoho Campaigns integrates with a variety of third-party applications, including Zoho CRM,

Salesforce, and Shopify, allowing businesses to sync their customer data and create targeted campaigns based on customer behavior.

In terms of pricing, Zoho Campaigns offers a variety of plans to fit the needs and budgets of businesses of all sizes. The plans range from a free plan that allows businesses to send up to 12,000 emails per month to a premium plan that includes advanced features such as A/B testing and advanced reporting.

Overall, Zoho Campaigns is a powerful and flexible email marketing automation tool that provides businesses with the features and functionality they need to create engaging and targeted email campaigns. With its easy-to-use interface, comprehensive automation features, and robust analytics capabilities, Zoho Campaigns is a great choice for businesses looking to improve their email marketing efforts.

D. Zoho Analytics

Zoho Analytics is a cloud-based business intelligence and analytics platform that enables users to create insightful dashboards, reports, and data visualizations. The platform is designed to help organizations of all sizes make data-driven decisions by consolidating data from various sources, analyzing it, and presenting it in a user-friendly format.

One of the main features of Zoho Analytics is its ability to integrate with over 500 data sources, including popular databases like MySQL, Oracle, and Microsoft SQL Server, as well as cloud services such as Google Drive, Dropbox, and Salesforce. This means that users can easily import data from different sources, eliminating the need for manual data entry and reducing the risk of errors.

Once data has been imported into Zoho Analytics, users can use a variety of tools to analyze it. These include pivot tables, charts, and graphs, as well as statistical functions and predictive analytics. Users can also create custom formulas and calculations to perform more complex analyses.

Zoho Analytics also offers a range of collaboration features, allowing teams to work together on data analysis projects. Users can share dashboards and reports with colleagues, set up data alerts to notify team members of changes in data, and even collaborate in real-time using the platform's built-in chat functionality.

Another key feature of Zoho Analytics is its ability to automate data analysis workflows. Users can create automated reports and dashboards that update in real-time as new data is added, eliminating the need for manual data updates and streamlining the analysis process.

Zoho Analytics also provides users with a range of customization options, allowing them to create branded reports and dashboards that align with their organization's branding. Users can choose from a range of templates, customize colors and fonts, and add logos and other branding elements to their reports and dashboards.

In terms of pricing, Zoho Analytics offers a range of plans to suit different business needs and budgets. There is a free plan that allows users to create up to two databases and includes basic reporting features. Paid plans start at $22 per month and offer more advanced features like predictive analytics and custom dashboards.

Overall, Zoho Analytics is a powerful and flexible platform that offers a range of features to help organizations of all sizes make data-driven decisions. With its ability to integrate with a wide range of data sources, powerful analytics tools, collaboration features, and customization options, it is a great choice for businesses looking to improve their data analysis capabilities.

E. Zoho Forms

Zoho Forms is a cloud-based form builder tool that allows businesses and individuals to create and publish customized forms for various purposes. With its intuitive drag-and-drop interface and extensive customization options, Zoho Forms makes it easy for anyone to create professional-looking forms without any coding experience.

Features:

- Drag-and-drop form builder: Zoho Forms offers an intuitive drag-and-drop interface that allows users to create custom forms easily. Users can drag and drop form fields, change the layout, and customize the design of their forms.

- Pre-built templates: Zoho Forms offers a wide range of pre-built templates that users can choose from. These templates cover different categories, including business, education, healthcare, non-profit, and more.

- Multi-page forms: With Zoho Forms, users can create multi-page forms, allowing them to organize their questions and responses better. This feature is particularly useful for long surveys and questionnaires.

- Conditional logic: Zoho Forms offers conditional logic that allows users to customize the flow of their forms based on the responses they receive. This feature allows users to create personalized forms that are tailored to the needs of each respondent.

- Payment integration: Zoho Forms integrates with various payment gateways, including PayPal, Stripe, and Authorize.net, making it easy for users to accept payments through their forms.

- Custom branding: Zoho Forms allows users to customize their forms with their brand logo, colors, and fonts, ensuring that their forms are consistent with their brand identity.

- Mobile app: Zoho Forms offers a mobile app that allows users to access their forms on-the-go. The app supports offline data collection, allowing users to collect data even when they are not connected to the internet.

- Integration with other Zoho apps: Zoho Forms integrates with other Zoho apps, including Zoho CRM, Zoho Desk, and Zoho Campaigns, making it easy for users to manage their data and automate their workflows.

Benefits:

- Easy to use: Zoho Forms is designed to be user-friendly, allowing anyone to create professional-looking forms without any coding experience.

- Customizable: With its extensive customization options, Zoho Forms allows users to create forms that match their brand identity and meet their specific needs.

- Saves time: Zoho Forms allows users to automate their workflows, saving them time and reducing manual data entry errors.

- Cost-effective: Zoho Forms is a cost-effective solution, offering various pricing plans that cater to the needs of businesses of all sizes.

- Mobile-friendly: Zoho Forms is designed to be mobile-friendly, allowing users to collect data on-the-go.

- Secure: Zoho Forms offers various security features, including SSL encryption, captcha verification, and IP blocking, ensuring that user data is protected.

Overall, Zoho Forms is a powerful tool that allows businesses and individuals to create customized forms quickly and easily. With its intuitive drag-and-drop interface, extensive customization options, and various features, Zoho Forms is an excellent solution for anyone looking to create professional-looking forms without any coding experience. Whether you need to create a survey, a contact form, or a registration form, Zoho Forms is an excellent choice that will save you time, money, and effort.

F. Zoho Sign

Zoho Sign is a cloud-based digital signature solution that allows businesses to sign, send, and manage legally binding documents digitally. It is a part of Zoho's suite of business applications, which includes Zoho CRM, Zoho Books, and Zoho One.

Zoho Sign helps businesses streamline their document workflows by eliminating the need for printing, signing, scanning, and mailing physical documents. It is designed to be easy to use, with a user-friendly interface and intuitive workflows.

Key Features of Zoho Sign

- Electronic Signature: Zoho Sign allows users to sign documents electronically, either by drawing their signature using a mouse or trackpad, uploading an image of their signature, or using a pre-defined signature font.

- Document Templates: Users can create reusable templates for frequently used documents, such as contracts, NDAs, and purchase orders, which can be edited and signed by multiple parties.

- Workflow Automation: Zoho Sign allows users to set up automated workflows for document signing, which can include multiple signers and approvers, notifications, reminders, and deadline tracking.

- Secure Document Storage: Signed documents are securely stored in the cloud, with access controls and audit trails to ensure compliance with regulatory requirements.

- Integrations: Zoho Sign integrates with a range of popular business applications, including Zoho CRM, Zoho Books, Google Drive, Dropbox, and Salesforce, among others.

Benefits of Zoho Sign

- Time and Cost Savings: Zoho Sign eliminates the need for printing, signing, and mailing physical documents, which can save businesses time and money.

- Improved Efficiency: Automated workflows and document templates can help businesses streamline their document signing processes, reducing the time and effort required to manage paperwork.

- Increased Security: Zoho Sign provides secure, encrypted document storage, access controls, and audit trails, which can help businesses ensure compliance with regulatory requirements and protect sensitive data.

- Enhanced Collaboration: Zoho Sign allows multiple parties to sign and edit documents online, improving collaboration and communication among team members and clients.

- Improved Customer Experience: Zoho Sign enables businesses to offer a more convenient and efficient signing experience for their customers, which can help improve customer satisfaction and loyalty.

Overall, Zoho Sign is a powerful digital signature solution that can help businesses streamline their document signing processes and improve their overall efficiency. With its user-friendly interface, robust feature set, and seamless integrations with other popular business applications, Zoho Sign is an excellent choice for businesses looking to simplify their paperwork and enhance their digital workflows.

V. ZOHO INTEGRATIONS

A. Integrating with Third-party Applications

Zoho is a powerful suite of cloud-based applications that can help businesses streamline their processes and increase productivity. While Zoho offers a wide range of built-in integrations, businesses often need to integrate Zoho with third-party applications to fully realize its potential. In this section, we will explore the benefits of integrating Zoho with third-party applications, the different methods of integration, and best practices for a successful integration.

Benefits of Integrating Zoho with Third-party Applications

Integrating Zoho with third-party applications can provide a wide range of benefits for businesses, including:

1. Increased Efficiency - Integrating Zoho with third-party applications can eliminate manual

data entry and streamline business processes. This can save time and increase productivity, allowing businesses to focus on more important tasks.

2. Improved Data Accuracy - Integrating Zoho with third-party applications can ensure that data is accurate and up-to-date across all systems. This can prevent errors and improve decision-making.

3. Enhanced Collaboration - Integrating Zoho with third-party applications can improve collaboration between different departments and teams. This can lead to better communication, more efficient workflows, and improved overall performance.

4. Expanded Functionality - Integrating Zoho with third-party applications can expand the functionality of both systems, allowing businesses to accomplish tasks that were not previously possible.

Methods of Integration

There are several methods of integrating Zoho with third-party applications, including:

1. API Integration - API integration allows businesses to connect Zoho with third-party applications by using APIs (Application Programming Interfaces) to exchange data between systems. This method requires some programming knowledge but is the most flexible and customizable option.

2. Zapier Integration - Zapier is a cloud-based integration platform that allows businesses to connect Zoho with over 3,000 other applications without any coding required. This method is easy to set up and can automate many tasks.

3. Webhooks Integration - Webhooks allow businesses to receive real-time notifications from third-party applications when certain events occur. This method can be used to trigger actions in Zoho based on events in other systems.

4. Middleware Integration - Middleware is software that connects different systems together. This method can be used to connect Zoho with multiple third-party applications, allowing businesses to centralize their data and automate tasks across systems.

Best Practices for Integration

To ensure a successful integration between Zoho and third-party applications, businesses should follow these best practices:

1. Define Objectives - Before starting the integration process, businesses should define their objectives and determine what they want to achieve by integrating Zoho with third-party applications.

2. Choose the Right Integration Method - Businesses should choose the integration method that best fits their needs and technical capabilities. For example, API integration is the most flexible but requires programming knowledge, while Zapier integration is easy to set up but has some limitations.

3. Test the Integration - Before going live, businesses should thoroughly test the integration to ensure that it works as expected and does not cause any issues.

4. Train Employees - Once the integration is live, businesses should train employees on how to use it and ensure that they understand the benefits of the integration.

5. Monitor and Optimize - Businesses should regularly monitor the integration and optimize it as needed to ensure that it continues to meet their needs and goals.

Overall, integrating Zoho with third-party applications can provide businesses with many benefits, including increased efficiency, improved data accuracy, enhanced collaboration, and expanded functionality. By choosing the right integration method, following best practices, and regularly monitoring and optimizing the integration, businesses can ensure a successful integration that helps them achieve their goals and improve their performance.

B. Using APIs for Custom Integrations

In today's interconnected world, APIs (Application Programming Interfaces) have become essential for businesses to achieve a seamless flow of data and information between various systems and applications. APIs are sets of protocols, tools, and standards used to build software applications and enable them to communicate with each other.

Using APIs for custom integrations is a popular way to connect different software systems, automate processes, and improve productivity. Custom integrations allow businesses to tailor their workflows to specific needs and optimize their operations.

Here's how to use APIs for custom integrations:

- **Understand the API documentation**

Before you can start using an API, you need to understand how it works. API documentation provides a detailed description of the API, including how to access it, what data it can provide, and how to format requests and responses. Make sure to read the documentation carefully and familiarize yourself with the API's endpoints and parameters.

- **Choose the right API**

There are many APIs available, each with its own features and limitations. When choosing an API for your custom integration, consider factors such as data quality, API reliability, and pricing. Make sure to choose an API that meets your specific needs and can provide the data you require for your integration.

- **Authenticate your API requests**

Most APIs require authentication to ensure that only authorized users can access the data. There are several ways to authenticate API requests, including OAuth, API keys, and basic authentication. Make sure to follow the authentication process specified in the API documentation to ensure that your requests are properly authorized.

- **Format your API requests**

API requests typically use the HTTP protocol and are formatted using a specific syntax, such as JSON or XML. Make sure to format your requests correctly, including the correct endpoint, HTTP method, and request body. If you are using a programming language, there may be libraries or frameworks available to help you format your requests.

- **Handle API responses**

API responses can vary depending on the API and the specific request. Responses may be in JSON, XML, or another format, and may include a variety of data such as text, images, or structured data. Make sure to handle API responses properly, including error handling and parsing the response data to extract the information you need.

- **Test and debug your integration**

Before deploying your custom integration, it is important to test and debug it thoroughly. Use test data and edge cases to ensure that your integration can handle a variety of scenarios. If you encounter errors or issues, use the API documentation and debugging tools to help identify and resolve the problem.

- **Monitor and maintain your integration**

Once your custom integration is live, it is important to monitor it regularly to ensure that it continues to function correctly. Set up alerts and monitoring tools to help identify issues or errors as soon as possible. As APIs and other services may change over time, make sure to keep your integration up to date and make any necessary changes or updates as needed.

In this section, we will discuss the benefits of using APIs for custom integrations and the steps involved in building custom integrations.

Benefits of using APIs for custom integrations

1. Streamlined Workflow: APIs make it easier to integrate various software systems and streamline workflows. Instead of manually transferring data between systems, APIs automate the transfer process, saving time and reducing the risk of errors.

2. Improved Productivity: Integrating systems with APIs can significantly improve productivity by eliminating redundant processes and automating manual tasks. This allows employees to focus on higher-value tasks and improve the overall efficiency of the organization.

3. Scalability: APIs are designed to be scalable, meaning they can handle large volumes of data and traffic. This makes them ideal for businesses that are growing or experiencing fluctuations in demand.

4. Cost-Effective: Building custom integrations with APIs can be cost-effective as it eliminates the need for expensive middleware and reduces the time and resources required to manage data transfers between systems.

5. Competitive Advantage: Custom integrations can give businesses a competitive advantage by enabling them to customize their workflows to specific needs and optimize their operations.

Steps involved in building custom integrations

1. Identify the systems to be integrated: The first step in building custom integrations is to identify the systems that need to be integrated. This includes identifying the data to be transferred between systems and the frequency of data transfers.

2. Select the appropriate API: Once the systems have been identified, the next step is to select the appropriate API. This involves evaluating

the functionality of different APIs and selecting the one that best meets the organization's needs.

3. Develop the integration: The next step is to develop the integration. This involves writing code to connect the systems and transfer data between them. This step may require the assistance of a developer or development team.

4. Test the integration: After the integration has been developed, it is important to test it thoroughly to ensure that it is working as intended. This involves testing for errors, bugs, and compatibility issues.

5. Deploy the integration: Once the integration has been tested and is working correctly, it can be deployed. This involves configuring the integration to run automatically and setting up any necessary permissions and security protocols.

6. Monitor the integration: After the integration has been deployed, it is important to monitor it regularly to ensure that it continues to function correctly. This involves monitoring for errors, performance issues, and security breaches.

Overall, using APIs for custom integrations can significantly improve productivity, streamline workflows, and provide a competitive advantage for businesses. By following the steps outlined above, businesses can successfully build custom integrations that meet their specific needs and optimize their operations.

VI. SECURITY AND COMPLIANCE

A. Data Security

Data security is an essential aspect of any organization that handles sensitive information, such as customer data, financial data, and intellectual property. Zoho, a cloud-based software company that offers a range of business applications, recognizes the importance of data security and offers several features and measures to ensure the protection of its users' data.

Here are some ways Zoho ensures data security:

1. Encryption: Zoho uses AES 256-bit encryption for data in transit and at rest. This ensures that data is encrypted both during transmission between the user's device and Zoho's servers and when stored on their servers. This encryption standard is considered to be one of the strongest and most secure available.

2. Multi-Factor Authentication: Zoho offers multi-factor authentication (MFA) to its users to add an additional layer of security to their accounts. This requires users to provide two or more pieces of evidence to authenticate their identity, such as a password and a one-time code generated by an app. This reduces the risk of unauthorized access to user accounts.

3. User Roles and Permissions: Zoho allows organizations to create user roles and permissions, ensuring that only authorized users have access to sensitive data. This helps to prevent data breaches caused by human error or internal threats.

4. Data Backup and Recovery: Zoho ensures that user data is regularly backed up and stored in multiple locations. This helps to ensure data availability in the event of a disaster, such as a server failure or natural calamity. Zoho also provides the option for users to download their data for additional backup and recovery measures.

5. Access Logs: Zoho provides access logs that allow users to see who has accessed their data and when. This helps users to monitor their data and identify any unauthorized access attempts.

6. Data Centers: Zoho uses multiple data centers located in different regions to ensure data availability and resilience. These data centers are designed to meet international security and compliance standards, such as SOC 2 Type II and ISO 27001.

7. Compliance: Zoho complies with several international data protection and privacy regulations, such as GDPR, HIPAA, and CCPA. This ensures that user data is protected and processed in accordance with the highest standards of data protection.

Overall, Zoho offers several features and measures to ensure data security, including encryption, multi-factor authentication, user roles and permissions, data backup and recovery, access logs, data centers, and compliance with international regulations. These features provide users with the assurance that their sensitive data is protected and secure.

B. Data Privacy

Data privacy is a crucial aspect of modern-day business operations, and it involves protecting sensitive information from unauthorized access or use. Zoho is a software company that offers a suite of cloud-based business tools to help organizations manage their data more efficiently. In this section, we will explore how Zoho handles data privacy and why it's essential for businesses to prioritize data privacy in their operations.

Firstly, Zoho recognizes the importance of data privacy and security, and it has implemented measures to ensure that its users' data is protected at all times. The company is compliant with various data privacy regulations such as the GDPR, CCPA, and HIPAA, and it has obtained certifications such as ISO 27001 and SOC 2 Type II. These certifications demonstrate Zoho's commitment to data privacy and security and give users peace of mind that their data is in safe hands.

Zoho also provides various features that enable users to maintain control over their data. For instance, users can choose to encrypt their data, control who can access it, and monitor data usage through audit logs. Additionally, Zoho's apps allow users to export their data and delete it if necessary, ensuring that users maintain control over their data at all times.

Another important aspect of data privacy is ensuring that data is not misused or mishandled by third-party service providers. Zoho has implemented various measures to ensure that its partners and service providers also comply with data privacy regulations and standards. For instance, Zoho conducts regular audits and assessments of its partners to ensure that they adhere to its data privacy policies and standards. Additionally, Zoho has implemented contractual agreements that require its partners to maintain the same level of data privacy and security as Zoho.

Zoho also provides users with various resources to help them understand data privacy and the steps they can take to protect their data. For instance, Zoho provides users with privacy policies and terms of service that outline how it handles data and how users can maintain control over their data. Additionally, Zoho's customer support team is available to answer any questions users may have about data privacy and security.

Overall, data privacy is essential for businesses to maintain the trust of their customers and protect sensitive information from unauthorized access or use. Zoho is committed to data privacy and security, and it has implemented various measures to ensure that its users' data is protected at all times. By using Zoho's suite of business tools, businesses can rest assured that their data is in safe hands and maintain control over their data at all times.

C. Compliance

Zoho is a cloud-based software company that provides a suite of business applications designed to help organizations streamline their operations and improve their overall productivity. Some of the popular products offered by Zoho include CRM, HR management, accounting, project management, and collaboration tools.

To ensure the security and privacy of data stored in its applications, Zoho follows strict compliance standards and regulations. In this section, we will discuss compliance with Zoho and the measures taken by the company to ensure the security of its customers' data.

1. GDPR Compliance:

Zoho is compliant with the General Data Protection Regulation (GDPR), which is a European Union regulation that came into effect on May 25, 2018. The GDPR governs the collection, storage, and processing of personal data of EU citizens, regardless of where the data is processed. Zoho's compliance with GDPR ensures that customer data is processed in accordance with the highest standards of privacy and data protection.

2. HIPAA Compliance:

Zoho is also compliant with the Health Insurance Portability and Accountability Act (HIPAA), which is a US federal law that sets standards for the protection of sensitive patient health information. This compliance allows Zoho to offer its services to healthcare organizations, which must comply with HIPAA regulations.

3. ISO/IEC 27001 Certification:

Zoho has also obtained ISO/IEC 27001 certification, which is a globally recognized standard for information security management. This certification demonstrates that Zoho has implemented and maintains an information security management system (ISMS) that meets the requirements of the standard.

4. PCI DSS Compliance:

Zoho is also compliant with the Payment Card Industry Data Security Standard (PCI DSS), which is a set of security standards designed to ensure that all companies that accept, process, store or transmit credit card information maintain a secure environment. This compliance allows Zoho to process payments and credit card transactions securely.

5. SOC 2 Compliance:

Zoho has also obtained Service Organization Control 2 (SOC 2) compliance, which is a widely recognized auditing standard developed by the American Institute of Certified Public Accountants (AICPA). This compliance ensures that Zoho has adequate controls in place to protect the security, availability, and confidentiality of customer data.

6. Privacy Shield Certification:

Zoho is also certified under the EU-US Privacy Shield Framework, which is a framework designed to facilitate the transfer of personal data from the European Union to the United States. This certification demonstrates that Zoho has implemented adequate data protection measures to ensure the privacy of EU citizens' personal data.

In addition to complying with these regulations and standards, Zoho also has various security measures (explained above) in place to protect customer data, such as data encryption, regular data backups, and multi-factor authentication. Zoho also employs a team of security experts who continuously monitor its systems for any potential security threats or vulnerabilities.

Overall, compliance with Zoho is of utmost importance, especially for organizations that handle sensitive data. With its robust compliance framework, Zoho ensures that its customers' data is protected at all times and that the company complies with the relevant regulations and standards.

VII. ZOHO SUPPORT AND RESOURCES

A. Customer Support

Zoho Customer Support is a comprehensive customer service solution that provides businesses with the tools they need to manage their customer interactions and improve customer satisfaction. It is part of the larger Zoho suite of business applications, which includes everything from accounting software to marketing automation tools.

Zoho Customer Support is designed to help businesses of all sizes to streamline their customer service operations and improve the overall customer experience. It is an all-in-one platform that provides businesses with a range of features, including ticket management, live chat, social media integration, and more.

One of the key features of Zoho Customer Support is its ticket management system. This allows businesses to track and manage customer inquiries and issues from a centralized dashboard. Tickets can be created automatically from email, social media, and other channels, and they can be assigned to specific agents or teams for resolution.

Another important feature of Zoho Customer Support is its live chat capabilities. Businesses can add a live chat widget to their website, allowing customers to get help in real-time. Agents can respond to chat requests from the same dashboard as their tickets, making it easy to manage multiple channels of communication.

Zoho Customer Support also offers social media integration, allowing businesses to monitor and respond to customer inquiries and complaints on popular social media platforms like Twitter and Facebook. This helps businesses to stay on top of customer feedback and address issues before they escalate.

Other notable features of Zoho Customer Support include a knowledge base for self-service support, automation tools for ticket routing and escalation, and robust reporting and analytics capabilities for tracking customer satisfaction and agent performance.

Zoho Customer Support is available as part of the larger Zoho suite of business applications, which includes CRM, marketing automation, project management, and more. This makes it easy for businesses to integrate their customer service operations with their overall business strategy and workflow.

In terms of pricing, Zoho Customer Support offers a range of plans to suit businesses of all sizes and budgets. The most basic plan starts at $12 per user per month, while more advanced plans include features like multichannel support and advanced analytics.

Overall, Zoho Customer Support is a comprehensive customer service solution that offers a range of features to help businesses manage their customer interactions and improve customer satisfaction. Its ticket management system, live chat capabilities, and social media integration make it a powerful tool for businesses looking to provide top-notch customer support.

B. Documentation and Help Center

Zoho Documentation and Help Center is a comprehensive resource center for users of Zoho's suite of business software solutions. The platform provides access to a wealth of information and resources, including articles, tutorials, videos, and community forums, to help users get the most out of their Zoho experience.

The platform offers support for a wide range of Zoho products, including CRM, SalesIQ, Projects, Books, Inventory, Recruit, and more. Users can access the Zoho Documentation and Help Center from within their Zoho application, or by visiting the Zoho website.

The platform is designed to be user-friendly and intuitive, with a clean and modern interface that makes it easy to find the information you need. Users can search for articles and resources using keywords, browse topics by category, or access the community forums to ask questions and get answers from other Zoho users.

One of the key features of the Zoho Documentation and Help Center is its extensive library of articles and tutorials. These resources cover a wide range of topics, from getting started with a new Zoho product to advanced features and customization options. The articles are written in clear and concise language, with step-by-step instructions and screenshots to help users follow along.

In addition to articles and tutorials, the Zoho Documentation and Help Center also offers a range of videos and webinars. These resources provide a more interactive and engaging learning experience, and cover topics such as product demos, best practices, and tips and tricks for using Zoho products more effectively.

Another valuable resource offered by the Zoho Documentation and Help Center is the community forums. These forums provide a platform for users to ask questions, share their experiences, and connect with other Zoho users. The forums are moderated by Zoho staff, ensuring that users receive accurate and helpful answers to their questions.

Overall, the Zoho Documentation and Help Center is a valuable resource for users of Zoho's suite of business software solutions. Whether you're a new user looking to get started with a Zoho product, or an experienced user looking for tips and best practices, the platform offers a wealth of information and resources to help you get the most out of your Zoho experience.

C. Community Forum

Zoho Community Forum is an online platform where users of Zoho products can interact with each other and exchange knowledge and ideas. It is a hub for Zoho users to ask questions, share best practices, and offer advice to other users. The forum is designed to promote collaboration, foster a sense of community, and provide a platform for Zoho users to help each other.

The Zoho Community Forum has a user-friendly interface that makes it easy to navigate and search for information. The forum is divided into different categories such as Zoho CRM, Zoho Books, Zoho Projects, Zoho Creator, Zoho Desk, and more. Each category has sub-forums dedicated to specific topics related to the product.

One of the benefits of using the Zoho Community Forum is the wealth of information available. Users can search for answers to their questions in the existing threads, or they can start a new thread and ask their question. Often, other users will jump in and offer advice or share their experiences.

The Zoho Community Forum is also a great place to stay up-to-date with the latest developments and updates from Zoho. Zoho product managers and developers often post updates on the forum, including new features, bug fixes, and other announcements. This ensures that Zoho users are always informed about the latest developments and can take advantage of new features as soon as they become available.

Another benefit of the Zoho Community Forum is that it fosters a sense of community among Zoho users. The forum is a place where users can connect with each other and share their experiences. It is not uncommon for users to form relationships and collaborate on projects together.

One of the most valuable aspects of the Zoho Community Forum is the customer support. Zoho has a team of support specialists who monitor the forum and provide assistance to users who need it. This means that users can get help from Zoho support staff as well as other users, creating a collaborative and supportive environment.

Overall, the Zoho Community Forum is a valuable resource for Zoho users. It provides a platform for users to ask questions, share knowledge, and collaborate with each other. The forum is easy to use and offers a wealth of information, making it an essential tool for anyone using Zoho products.

D. Training and Certification

Zoho is a leading cloud-based software provider that offers a wide range of business applications, including customer relationship management (CRM), human resources management (HRM), accounting, and marketing automation, among others. As Zoho's applications become more popular, it is essential for users to obtain training and certification to fully utilize the software's capabilities. This section will provide an overview of Zoho training and certification programs, including their benefits and how to get certified.

Zoho Training Programs

Zoho offers several training programs to help users learn how to use their software effectively. The training programs are designed to cater to different levels of users, from beginners to advanced users.

1. Zoho One Training: Zoho One is a comprehensive suite of over 50 applications designed to help businesses manage their operations more efficiently. Zoho One training

is an excellent option for users who want to learn how to use the entire suite of applications effectively. The training program includes self-paced modules, webinars, and instructor-led sessions.

2. Zoho CRM Training: Zoho CRM is a powerful customer relationship management software that helps businesses manage their sales pipeline, customer data, and communication effectively. Zoho CRM training is designed to help users understand the software's features and capabilities, such as lead management, deal management, and automation.

3. Zoho Books Training: Zoho Books is an accounting software designed for small businesses. Zoho Books training helps users understand the software's features, including invoicing, expense tracking, and inventory management.

4. Zoho Creator Training: Zoho Creator is a low-code platform that allows users to create

custom applications without any coding knowledge. Zoho Creator training is designed to help users create and deploy custom applications using the platform's drag-and-drop interface.

5. Zoho Campaigns Training: Zoho Campaigns is a marketing automation software that helps businesses create and manage email campaigns effectively. Zoho Campaigns training helps users understand the software's features, such as email templates, A/B testing, and analytics.

Benefits of Zoho Training Programs

Zoho training programs offer several benefits to users, including:

1. Improved Productivity: Zoho training programs help users learn how to use the software's features effectively, which can improve their productivity and efficiency.

2. Better ROI: By learning how to use Zoho's software effectively, businesses can generate

better returns on their investment in the software.

3. Increased Collaboration: Zoho training programs can help team members collaborate more effectively by providing them with a common understanding of the software's features and capabilities.

4. Better Customer Service: Zoho training programs can help users understand how to use the software's customer service features effectively, such as ticket management and knowledge base.

Zoho Certification Programs

Zoho certification programs are designed to help users demonstrate their proficiency in using Zoho software. There are several certification programs available, including:

1. Zoho CRM Certified Consultant: This certification program is designed for consultants who help businesses implement and customize Zoho CRM software.

2. Zoho Books Certified Advisor: This certification program is designed for accountants and bookkeepers who provide financial consulting services to businesses.

3. Zoho Creator Certified Developer: This certification program is designed for developers who create custom applications using Zoho Creator.

4. Zoho Campaigns Certified Consultant: This certification program is designed for consultants who help businesses implement and customize Zoho Campaigns software for their marketing needs.

5. Zoho Certified Trainer: This certification program is designed for individuals who want to become certified trainers for Zoho software. The program covers training techniques, best practices, and Zoho software expertise.

Benefits of Zoho Certification Programs

Zoho certification programs offer several benefits to individuals and businesses, including:

1. Enhanced Credibility: Zoho certification programs help individuals and businesses demonstrate their expertise in using Zoho software, which can enhance their credibility with clients and customers.

2. Improved Career Opportunities: Zoho certification can lead to better career

opportunities for individuals, as it demonstrates their proficiency in using Zoho software, which is in high demand among businesses.

3. Increased Revenue: Zoho certification can lead to increased revenue for businesses, as it demonstrates their expertise in using Zoho software, which can attract more clients.

4. Access to Zoho Support: Zoho certification provides access to Zoho support, which can help individuals and businesses resolve software-related issues more quickly.

How to Get Zoho Certified

To get Zoho certified, individuals must complete the certification program and pass the certification exam. Zoho certification programs are available online, and individuals can register for the program through the Zoho website. The certification exam is typically a multiple-choice test, and individuals must score a passing grade to receive the certification.

Overall, Zoho training and certification programs offer several benefits to users and businesses. By completing the training program, individuals can learn how to use Zoho software effectively, which can lead to improved productivity, better ROI, and increased collaboration. Zoho certification programs demonstrate individuals' proficiency in using Zoho software, which can enhance their credibility, lead to better career opportunities, and increase revenue for businesses.

VIII. CONCLUSION

Zoho offers numerous benefits to businesses of all sizes. Its integrated suite of applications, scalability, user-friendly interface, comprehensive customer support, data security, cost-effectiveness, and mobile app make it an excellent choice for businesses looking to manage their day-to-day operations efficiently and effectively.

www.ingramcontent.com/pod-product-compliance
Lightning Source LLC
Chambersburg PA
CBHW070540220526
45467CB00003B/1004